Effective Leadership Management

An Integration of Styles, Skills & Character for Today's CEOs

by

Dr. Michael Adewale Adeniyi, Ph.D.

authorHOUSE®

AuthorHouse™
1663 Liberty Drive, Suite 200
Bloomington, IN 47403
www.authorhouse.com
Phone: 1-800-839-8640

First published by AuthorHouse 10/9/2007

ISBN: 978-1-4259-7597-5 (sc)
ISBN: 978-1-4259-7598-2 (hc)

Printed in the United States of America
Bloomington, Indiana

This book is printed on acid-free paper.

Dedication

To
God the Father, Christ the Son and the Holy Spirit
"who has given me strength to do all things." Phillipians 4:13

To
My Family, Grace, Mary, Stephen, Andrew, & Michelle
Their Patience, Love, and Understanding Made this Book a Possibility

&
All *our* staff at Blessed Home Care and Assisted Living Facility
For their hardworking, dedication, and compassionate caring.

Table of Contents

INTRODUCTION

People follow leaders they know -- leaders who care. People follow and trust leaders with character. People follow and respect leaders who are competent. People follow and approach leaders who are consistent and people follow and admire leaders with commitment.

When he was installed as president of Harvard University in October 2001, Lawrence Summers delivered a speech in which he declared that "in this new century, nothing will matter more than the education of future leaders and the development of new ideas." (Summers, 2001). In this single sentence the new head of Harvard made at least two important assumptions: that people can be educated in ways that relate to being leaders, and in ways that relate to being good leaders.

This kind of positive thinking explains why leadership education has become a big business. The "leadership industry" is dedicated to the proposition that leadership is a subject that should be studied and a skill that should be taught. To meet the increasing demand for leadership education and training, many experts have emerged. These leadership scholars, teachers, consultants, trainers, and coaches work on the optimistic assumption that to develop leaders is to develop a valuable human resource.

The academic work that supports the leadership generally shares this positive bias. The titles of many of the best and most popular leadership books of the past twenty years send messages that make the point. Targeted primarily at those in the corporate sector, they include Thomas J. Peters and Robert H. Waterman's *In Search of Excellence: Lessons from America's Best-Run Companies*; (Peters & Waterman, 1982). Rosabeth Moss Kanter's *The Change Masters: Innovation & Entrepreneurship in the American Corporation*; (Kanter, 1983). Warren Bennis and Burt Nanus's *Leaders: The Strategies for Taking Charge*; (Bennis & Nanus, 1985). John Kotter's *A Force for Change: How Leadership Differs from Management*; (Kotter, 1990). Noel Tichy's (Tichy & Cohen, 1997). And Jay Conger and Beth Benjamin's Building *The Leadership Engine: How Winning Companies Build Leaders at Every Level; Leaders: How Successful Companies Develop the Next Generation.* (Conger & Benjamin, 1999). Stephen Covey's *Seven Habits of Highly Effective People*; (Covey,

1990). Peter F. Drucker's *Management Challenges for the 21ˢᵗ Century*, (Drucker,1999), *On the Profession of Management*, (Drucker, 1998), and *Managing in the Next Society*, (Drucker, 2002). Each of these books assumes that people can learn to be leaders and that to be a leader is to be a person of competence and character.

On Monday you're doing what comes naturally, enjoying your job, running a project, talking and laughing with colleagues about life and work, and gossiping about how better management can be. Then on Tuesday, you are made a manager. You're a boss and a leader.

Suddenly, everything feels different. Leadership requires distinct behaviors and attitudes, and for many people, they debut with the job. Before you are a leader, success is all about growing yourself. When you become a leader, success is all about growing others.

Without question, there are lots of ways to be a leader. You need to look only as far as the freewheeling, straight-talking Herb Kelleher, who ran Southwest Airlines for thirty years, Microsoft's quiet innovator, Bill Gates, the Billionaire Next Door, Warren Buffet, and Donald Trump with Trump Foundation and the Apprentice, to know that leaders come in all varieties.

Leadership is not about getting the money or the fame or the accolades or the status. It is about one person making decisions and giving orders from a lofty perch, pulpit, or vacuum. It is not possible without a leader who genuinely cares about the cause and those behind it. It is not a dictatorship, but a fellowship.

Leadership is about serving, compassion, hard work, dedication, and tireless enthusiasm for what you're doing and for the people you're doing it with. Leader challenges, mediates, motivates, communicates and inspires. Sometimes with a shout, sometimes with a whisper, but always by example.

Over the past ten years, during my talks with managers, principals, superintendents, church presidents, university presidents, business owners, hospital administrators, physicians, and chief executive officers of various organizations, leadership issues such as integrity, personality, skills, concepts and character were discussed. In other words, how does a leader improve effectiveness and efficiency?.

Some new managers, for instance said that " I was just promoted and I've never run anything before. How can I be a good leader?"

Micromanagement often comes up as an area of concern, as in, "My boss feels as if he has to control everything - is that leadership or babysitting?" Similarly charisma gets a lot of queries; people ask, can you be introverted, quiet, or just plain shy and still get results out of your people?" Are you a weak leader because you are quiet, does not talk very often, and tends to control your emotion? If you have subordinates who are smarter than you how can you possibly appraise them?

These kinds of questions have pushed me to make sense of my own leadership experiences over ten years. Across the decade, circumstances varied widely. I led associations with ten, twenty and over fifty families. I led a health care facility with over two hundred beds as an assistant administrator. Worked as a licensee and administrator of a licensed assisted living facility for over ten years. I managed businesses that were dying and ones that were bursting with growth. There were acquisitions, divestitures, organizational crises, moments of unexpected luck, good economies and bad. And yet, some ways of leading always seemed to work. They became my principles or habits.

Leadership skills and positive mind-set apply everywhere, from the playground to the office of the CEO, because the laws of leadership are universal. They apply to every circumstance, grade school through retirement home. From the school system to the health care system. From the government court house to the private religious organization or church. And they work for everyone, from the quite and meek to the loud and sleek. Every man or woman. Boy or girl, can develop the qualities that make a great leader, whether you're rubbing elbows with the titans of industry or the common man.

When you place yourself out front in a leadership position, you invariably experience mental and physical highs and lows, triumphs and tragedies, that relate to your vision and all its attendant choices and decisions. In other words, you're going to face pressure, often of the full-court variety.

This pressure can keep you awake at night. Accepting ultimate responsibility for all matters in pursuit of turning vision into reality is a full-time job. Leaders need to know this, and to be prepared for sleepless nights and anxious hours.

The kind of leader who does not walk the talk probably does not lose sleep for concern about the product, the services, the staff, and other issues that a leader with integrity cares about. Unworthy leaders often do not even remember what they have said, instead walking in any direction that is convenient for them at any given moment.

Leadership is loaded with paradoxes of managing quarterly results and still do what's right for the organization five or ten years out. Any one can manage for the short term -- just keep squeezing the lemon (heads down). And anyone can manage for the long term -- just keep dreaming (heads up). You were made a leader because someone believed you could squeeze and dream at the same time. They saw in you a person with enough insight, experience, and rigor to balance the conflicting demands of short-and long-term results.

The need for leadership in this book applies to every area of human endeavor. All of us belong to groups and organizations of various kinds, ranging from the family, to the church, to the health care facility, to the university level, to the business corporation, and to other work place. Virtually every one of these groups and organizations maintains some kind of order, and some kind of order means some kind of leadership. Performing balancing acts everyday is leadership.

This book is divided into four major parts each dealing with components of leadership -- character, styles, skills, and service. *Character*, the leader's behavior or personality. *Styles*, the way a leader relates and does the job daily. *Skills*, performance which could be developed on the job. Putting these three together effectively will result in *serving leadership*. Blanchard and Miller (2004) indicated that "lack of character is still the nemesis of most leaders in our world today." Skills and styles are critical to effective leadership, but character is also. Many believe they can become effective leaders if they only had the skills or the styles. Others believe they can become great leaders if they could just develop their character. It takes skills, styles, character, and the spirit of serving to be effective, efficient, successful, productive, and to have positive results.

PART I
LEADERSHIP AND CHARACTER

"Wherever man goes to dwell, his character goes with him"
--African Proverb

CHAPTER ONE

LEADERSHIP PERSONALITY AND EFFECTIVENESS

"For the conduit of life, habits are more important than maxims, because a habit is a maxim verified. To take a new set of maxims for one's guide is not more than to change the title of a book, but to change one's habits is to change one's life. Life is only a tissue of habits"

--Frederic Amiel

"The formation of right habits is essential to your permanent security. They diminish your chance of falling when assailed, and they augment your chance of recovery when overthrown"

--John Tyndall

Our character, basically, is a composite of our habits. "Sow a thought, reap an action; sow an action, reap a habit; sow a habit, reap a character; sow a character, reap a destiny," the maxim goes. Habits are powerful factors in our lives. Because they are consistent, often unconscious patterns, they constantly, daily, express our character and produce our effectiveness . . . or ineffectiveness. As Horace Mann, the great educator, once said, "Habits are like a cable. We weave a strand of it everyday and soon it cannot be broken." (Covey, 1990).

Leadership Integrity

"There can be no friendship without confidence, and no confidence without integrity"

-- Samuel Johnson

"Integrity includes but goes beyond honesty. Honesty is telling the truth - conforming our words to reality. Integrity is conforming reality to our words - in other words, keeping promises and fulfilling expectation."

(Covey 1990). This requires an integrated character, a oneness, primarily with self but, also with life. One of the ways to manifest integrity is to be loyal to those who are not present. In doing so, we build the trust of those who are present.

Author and entrepreneur Byrd Baggett defines integrity as "doing what you said you would do, when you said you would do it, and how you said you would do it."

As a leader, one of your most vital jobs is to set the standards for those you intend to lead, whether you are the head of a household, the pastor of a church, leader of a charity organization, the captain of a team or club, the owner of a small business, the CEO of a large corporation, or the president of a country.

The hard part of it all is that you yourself need to live up to those standards. Every day! One of the most crucial promises a leader makes, whether he knows it or not, is that he'll consistently rise above the bar that he himself sets. In other words, a leader promises to "walk the talk."

If a leader does not walk the talk, he becomes a hypocrite, a liar, and a leader who does not deserve to be followed. A worthy leader should be prepared to walk a mile in the shoes of those who stand behind him. What I am suggesting here is the standards, strategies, policies, philosophies, and above all, integrity that need to be defined at the outset of-and modified if necessary throughout the life of -- any endeavor.

There are as many ways to lead as there are leaders. That's because leadership is based on personality as much as on anything else. One leader may be the strong, silent type while another can be dynamo of energy. The earnest and matter-of-fact straight shooter can be as effective as the imaginative and over-the-top visionary.

Dwight D. Eisenhower define the word integrity more lucidly when he said, "In order to be a leader a man must have followers. And to have followers, a man must have their confidence. Hence, the supreme quality for a leader is unquestionable integrity. Without it, no real success is possible, no matter whether it is in the church, basketball court, in an army, or in a corporation.

Trust can be earned by living a life infused with a strong sense of integrity. And integrity can be firmed up by fostering four characteristics. First is *congruity* -- practicing what you preach. Second is *responsibility* --

taking responsibility for your actions and admit your mistakes, apologize to all those offended and rectify the matter as soon as possible.

Third is *reliability* -- availability in the moments that matter. Being accessible in times of turmoil. Honoring your promises and commitments. And lastly, *honesty* -- telling the truth. Think the truth. Honest in words and in deed.

Emerson said: "The ancestor to every action is a thought." A leader's honesty has to be a constant policy at work or at play. Your actions in all areas of your life can affect your position as a leader, and you must be aware of this fact.

The character and personality ethic is the foundation of success -- things like integrity, simplicity, humility, fidelity, temperance, courage, justice, patience, industry, modesty, and the Golden Rule. Benjamin Franklin's autobiography is representative of that literature. It is, basically, the story of one man's effort to integrate certain principles and habits deep within his nature. The Character Ethics taught that there are basic principles of effective living, and that people can only experience true success and enduring happiness as they learn and integrate these principles into their basic character.

Modern success become more a function of personality, of public image, of attitudes and behaviors, skills and techniques, that lubricate the processes of human interaction. This Personality Ethic essentially took two paths: one was human and public relations techniques, and the other was positive mental attitude (PMA). Some of this philosophy was expressed in inspiring and sometimes valid maxims such as "Your attitude determines your altitude," "Smiling wins more friends than frowning," and "Whatever the mind of man can conceive and believe it can achieve." (Croce, 2004).

Other parts of the personality approach were clearly manipulative, even deceptive, encouraging people to use techniques to get other people to like them, or to fake interest in the hobbies of others to get out of them what they wanted, or to use the "power look," or to intimidate their way through life.

Some of these literature acknowledged character as an ingredient of success, but tended to compartmentalize it rather than recognize it as foundational and catalytic. Reference to the Character Ethic became mostly lip service; the basic trust was quick-fix influence techniques, power strategies, communication skills, and positive attitudes.

If I try to use human influence strategies and tactics of how to get other people to do what I want, to work better, to be more motivated, to like me and each other -- while my character is fundamentally flawed, marked by duplicity and insincerity -- then, in the long run, I cannot be successful. My duplicity will breed distrust, and everything I do -- even using so-called good human relations techniques -- will be perceived as manipulative. It simply makes no difference how good the rhetoric is or even how good the intentions are; if there or no trust, there is no foundation for permanent success. Only basic goodness gives life to technique.

To focus on technique is like cramming your way through school. You sometimes get by, perhaps even get good grades, but if you don't pay the price day in and day out, you never achieve true mastery of the subjects you study or develop an educated mind.

This principle is also true, ultimately, in human behavior, in human relationships. They, too are natural systems based on the law of the harvest. In the short run, in an artificial social system such as school, you may be able to get by if you learn how to manipulate the man-made rules, to "play the game." In most one-short or short-lived human interactions, you can use the Personality Ethic to get by and to make favorable impressions through charm and skill and pretending to be interested in other people's hobbies. You can pick up quick, easy techniques that may work in short-term situations. But secondary traits alone have no permanent worth in long-term relationships. Eventually, if there isn't deep integrity and fundamental character strength, the challenges of life will cause true motives to surface and human relationship failure will replace short-term success.

Many people with secondary greatness -- that is, social recognition for their talents--lack primary greatness or goodness in their character. Sooner or later, you'll see this in every long-term relationship they have, whether it is with a business associate, a spouse, a friend, or a teenage child going through an identity crisis. It is character that communicates most eloquently. As Emerson once put it, "What you are shouts so loudly in my ears I cannot hear what you say."

There are, of course, situations where people have character strength but they lack communication skills, and that undoubtedly affects the quality of relationships as well. But the effects are still secondary. What we are communicated far more eloquently that anything we say or do. We all know it. There are people we trust absolutely because we know their character. Whether they're eloquent or not, whether they have the human relations techniques or not, we trust them, and we work successfully with them.

In the words of William George Jordan, "Into the hands of every individual is given a marvelous power for good or evil -- the silent, unconscious, unseen influence of his life. This is simply the constant radiation of what man really is, not what he pretends to be."

To be a good leader, learn what it means to follow. To be an inspired leader, share of yourself. To be a great leader, develop the heart of the servant. The servant-leader tempers passion with compassion, inspires through his actions, and is willing to listen to and learn from those he leads. He keeps his door and his ears open, and knows when to close his mouth.

The servant-leader has a strong sense of empathy. He knows that whatever needs to be done is not beneath him, and that there should be no limit to sharing ideas, gripes, compliments, solutions, and dreams. He understands that people don't really care how much you know until they know how much you care.

Ultimately, an effective leader is willing to take responsibility, give endless support, cover other's backs, and keep the team moving forward. Effective Leadership in a Contemporary Society embody many of the fundamental principles of human effectiveness. These habits are basic; they are primary. They represent the internalization of correct principles upon which enduring happiness and success are based.

Principles Governing Leadership Effectiveness

The leader's character is based on the fundamental idea that there are principles that govern human effectiveness - natural laws in the human dimension that are just as real, just as unchanging and unarguably there as laws such as gravity are in the physical dimension.

An idea of the reality - and the impact - of these principles can be captured in another paradigm-shifting experience as told by Frank Koch in Proceedings. This is where reality is seen as superseded by his limited perception - a reality that is critical for us to understand in our daily lives as it was for the captain in the fog.

Principles are like lighthouses. They are natural laws that cannot be broken. As Cecil b. deMille observed of the principles contained in his monumental movie, *The Ten Commandments*, "It is impossible for us to break the law. We can only break ourselves against the law."

While individuals may look at their own lives and interactions in terms of paradigms or maps emerging out of their experience and conditioning, these maps are not the territory. They are a "subjective reality," only an attempt to describe the territory.

The "objective reality," or the territory itself, is composed of "lighthouse " principles that govern human growth and happiness -- natural laws that are woven into the fabric of every civilized society throughout history and comprise the roots of every family and institution that has endured and prospered. The degree to which our mental maps accurately describe the territory does not alter its existence.

The reality of such principles or natural laws becomes obvious to anyone who thinks deeply and examines the cycles of social history. These principles surface time and time again, and the degree to which people in a society recognize and live in harmony with them moves them toward either survival and stability or disintegration and destruction.

The principle referred to are not esoteric, mysterious, or "religious" ideas. There is not one principle taught in this book that is unique to any specific faith or religion, including my own. These principles are a part of most every major enduring religion, as well as enduring social philosophies and ethical systems. They are self-evident and can easily be validated by any individual. It's also most as if these principles or natural laws are part of the human condition, part of the human consciousness, part of the human conscience. They seem to exist in all human beings, regardless of social conditioning and loyalty to them, even though they might be submerged or numbered by such conditions or disloyalty.

I am referring to the principle of *fairness*, out of which our whole concept of equity and justice is developed. Little children seem to have an innate sense of the idea of fairness even apart from opposite conditioning experiences. There are vast differences in how fairness is defined and achieved, but there is almost universal awareness of the idea. Other examples would include *integrity* and *honesty*. They create the foundation of trust which essential to cooperation and long-term personal and interpersonal growth.

Another principle is *human dignity*. The basic concept in the United States Declaration of Independence speaks this value or principle. "We hold these truths to be self-evident: that all men are created equal and endowed by their Creator with certain inalienable rights, that among these are life, liberty and the pursuit of happiness."

Another principle is *service*, or the idea of making a contribution, Another is *quality* or *excellence*.

There is the principle of *potential*, the idea that we are embryonic and can grow and develop and release more and more potential, develop more and more talents. Highly related to *potential* is the principle *growth* -- the process of releasing potential and developing talents, with the accompanying need for principles such as *patience, nurturance,* and *encouragement*.

Principles are not *practices*. A practice is a specific activity or action. A practice that works in one circumstance will not necessarily work in another, as parents who have tried to raise a third and forth child exactly like they did the first and second can readily attest.

While practices are situationally specific, principles are deep, fundamental truths that have universal application. They apply to individuals, to marriages, to families, to private and public organizations of every kind. When these truths are internalized into habits, they empower people to create a wide variety of practices to deal with different situations.

Principles are not values. A gang of thieves can share values, but they are in violation of the fundamental principles we've talking about. Principles are the territory. Values are maps. When we value correct principles, we have truth - a knowledge of things as they are.

Principles are guidelines for human conduct that are proven to have enduring, permanent value. They're fundamental. They're essentially unarguable because they are self-evident. One way to quickly grasp the self-evident nature of principles is to simply consider the absurdity of attempting to live an effective life based on their opposites. I doubt that anyone would seriously consider unfairness, deceit, baseness, uselessness, mediocrity, or degeneration to be a solid foundation for lasting happiness and success.

The more closely our maps or paradigms are aligned with these principles or natural laws, the more accurate and functional they will be. Correct maps will infinitely impact our personal and interpersonal effectiveness far more than any amount of effort expended on changing our attitudes and behaviors.

The Genetic of Leadership

People are intrigued when they see good things happening in the lives of individuals, families, and organizations that are based on solid principles. They admire such personal strength and maturity, such as family unity and teamwork, such adaptive synergistic organizational culture. Their immediate request is very revealing of their basic paradigm. "How do you do it? Teach me the techniques." What they're really saying is, "Give me some quick fix advice or solution that will relieve the pain in my own situation."

They will find people who will meet their wants and teach these things; and for a short time, skills and techniques may appear to work. They may eliminate some of the cosmetic or acute problems through social aspirin and band-aids. But the underlying chronic condition remains, and eventually new acute symptoms will appear. The more people are into quick fix and focus on the acute problems and pain, the more that very approach contributes to the underlying chronic condition.

"I've taken course after course on effective management training. I expect a lot out of my employees and I work hard to be friendly toward them and to treat them right. But many leaders do not feel any loyalty from their staff. If some of these managers were to be home sick for a day, employees would probably spend most of their time gabbing at the water fountain. Why can't leaders train them to be independent and responsible - or find employees who can be?"

Rationalization tells me leadership could take some kind of dramatic action - shake things up, make heads roll - that would make these employees shape up and appreciate what they have. Or that leadership could find some motivational training program that would get them committed. Or even that the organization could hire new people that would do a better job.

But is it possible that under that apparently disloyal behaviors, these employees question whether leadership really act in their best interest? Do they feel like they are being treated as mechanical objects? Is there some truth to that? Deep inside, is that really the way leadership see them? Is there a chance the way leadership look at the people who work for them is part of the problem.

Effective leadership is not a set of separate or piecemeal psych-up formula. In harmony with the natural laws of growth, they provide an incremental, sequential, highly integrated approach to the development of personal and interpersonal effectiveness. Each of us begin life as an infant, totally dependent on others. We are directed, nurtured, and sustained by others. Without this nurturing, we would only live for a few hours or a few days at the most. Then gradually, over the ensuing months and years, we become more independent - physically, mentally, emotionally, and financially - until eventually we can essentially take care of ourselves, becoming inner-directed and self-reliant.

As we continue to grow and mature, we become increasingly aware that all of nature is interdependent, that there is an ecological system that governs nature, including society. We further discover that the higher reaches of our nature have to do with our relationships with others - that human life also is interdependent.

Our growth from infancy to adulthood is in accordance with natural law. And there are many dimensions to growth. Reaching our full physical maturity, for example, does not necessarily assure us of simultaneous emotional or mental maturity. On the other hand, a person's physical dependence does not mean that he or she is mentally or emotionally immature.

Attributes of Great and Effective Leaders

Katz and Kahn (1967) characterized an effective leader as a person who

1. Mediates and tempers the organizational requirements to the needs of persons in a manner that is organizationally enhancing (the facility assists employees having family crises through unplanned time off and other support)
2. Promotes group loyalty and personal ties (working for the facility becomes a personally satisfying experience)
3. Demonstrates care for individuals (knows each employee by name and something about that employee's interests) and
4. Relies on referent power (respect from employees and patients) rather than the power of legitimacy and sanctions alone.

Leadership is a lot like an iceberg. There are two primary components. What you see above the waterline and what you can't see, below the water. When the Titanic ship was wrecked on that faithful April 15, 1912 on her way from England to New York, it was not the ice berg on the surface that sunk the giant ship but the ice berg below the water level.

The same principle applies to leadership. "Leadership is more about what others do not see than what they do see." Below the waterline is the character or being of a leader. Above the waterline are the skills or doing of a leader.

For the purpose of this book, leadership will be defined as the integration of *character, knowledge, skill,* and *desire.* Character is your *being.* Knowledge is the theoretical paradigm, the *what to do* and the *why.* Skill is how you serve, the *how to do.* And desire is the motivation, the *want to do.* In order to make something a habit in our lives, we have to have all four.

I may be ineffective in my interactions with my work associates, my spouse, or my children because I constantly tell them what I think, but I never really listen to them. Unless I search out correct principles of human interaction, I may not even know I need to listen.

Even if I do know that in order to interact effectively with others I really need to listen to them. I may not have the skill. I may not know how to really listen deeply to another human being. But knowing I need to listen and knowing how to listen is not enough. Unless I want to listen, unless I have the desire, it won't be a habit in my life. Creating a habit requires work in all three dimensions.

The being/seeing change is an upward process - being changing seeing, which in turn changes being, and so forth, as we move in an upward spiral of growth. By working on knowledge, skill, and desire, we can break through to new levels of personal and interpersonal and leadership effectiveness as we break with old paradigms that may have been a source of pseudo-security for years.

It's sometimes a painful process. It's a change that has to be motivated by a higher purpose, by the willingness to subordinate what you think you want now for what you want later. But this process produces happiness, "the object and design of our existence." Happiness can be defined, in part at least, as the fruit of the desire and ability to sacrifice what we want now for what we want eventually.

Concepts of Efficiency and Effectiveness

Efficiency is the ability to produce the desired effect with a minimum of effort, expense, or waste (Webster's New World Dictionary, 2006). Efficiency can be measured by the ratio of effective work to the energy expended in producing it. In systems terms this simply means getting the maximum outputs with the minimum inputs (Pfeffer & Salanick, 1978).

Effectiveness is the power or ability to bring about the desired results. An organization that sets a goal of achieving excellence in customer care and then does so is said to be effective (Pfeffer & Salanick, 1978).

It may not, however, be efficiently achieving excellence of patient care. The facility may, for example, be employing a large number of employees to accomplish excellence in customer care. Yet studies in personnel reveal that when more people are placed on a work shift than are needed, the quality of care is not necessarily improved. The staff may simply divide the work up to lighten the load for everyone, or take more frequent breaks and not actually give additional attention to the customers. In this case, the too heavy staff to customer ratio may lead to both inefficiency and ineffectiveness (Robey, 1982).

The solution is to assign the optimum number of staff known to be needed to provide excellence in care to a specified number of customers and then manage their time so that the amount of work and quality are optimized. In this way, the manager achieves both efficiency (the desired effect with a minimum of effort, expense, or waste) and effectiveness (the desired results). Given enough resources and appropriate consultation, almost any manager, leader or administrator can achieve effectiveness. What is essential today is to be both effective and efficient.

The Effective Leaders should cultivate the habits of *effectiveness*. Because they are based on principles, they bring the maximum long-term beneficial results possible. They become the basis of a person's character, creating an empowering center of correct maps from which an individual can effectively solve problems, maximize opportunities, and continually learn and integrate other principles in an upward spiral of growth.

They are also habits of effectiveness because they are based on a paradigm of effectiveness that is in harmony with a natural law. In his book: *The 7 Habits of Highly Effective People*, (1990), Stephen R. Covey illustrates the effectiveness in the principle called the "P/PC Balance," P. for *production* of desired results - the golden eggs. PC for *production capability* - which is the ability or asset that produces the golden eggs.

According to Stephen, the fable is the story of a poor farmer who one day discovers in the nest of his pet goose a glittering golden egg. At first, he thinks it must be some kind of trick. But as he starts to throw the egg aside, he has second thoughts and takes it in to be appraised instead. The egg is pure gold! The farmer can't believe his good fortune. He becomes even more incredulous the following day when the experience is repeated. Day after day, he awakens to rush to the nest and find another golden egg. He becomes fabulously wealthy, it all seems too good to be true.

But with his increasing wealth comes greed and impatience. Unable to wait day after day for the golden eggs, the farmer decides he will kill the goose and get them all at once. But when he opens the goose, he find it empty. There are no golden eggs - and now there is no way to get any more. The farmer has destroyed the goose that produced them.

He suggests that within this fable is a natural law, a principle - the basic definition of effectiveness. Most people see effectiveness from the golden egg paradigm: the more you produce, the more you do, the more effective you are.

But as the story shows, true effectiveness is a function of two things: what is produced (the golden eggs) and the producing asset or capacity to produce (the goose). If you adopt a pattern of life that focuses on golden eggs and neglects the goose, you will soon be without the asset that produces golden eggs. On the contrary, if you only take care of the goose with no aim toward the golden eggs, you soon won't have the wherewithal to feed yourself or the goose.

In the book *"Wisdom for Young CEO,"* Barry Douglas (2004), states that effective leaders should have good moral principles by striving for excellence - delivering your best. Put your customer first. Know your customers, understand their needs, and surpass their expectations. Be passionate about what you do. Enthusiasm and energy are contagious. Never stop caring. Show concern and respect for every individual, regardless of position or title. Understand your role in the big picture. You are all part of a larger whole. Look for new and better ways to do things to continually raise your standards. Communicate. Voice your ideas, share your concerns, pass on what you know, and be honest. Be a team player. You are stronger when you work together. Listen when others speak. Good ideas can come from anywhere. Be flexible. Success depends upon a willingness to adapt when situations change. Pay attention to the details - little things do make a difference. Solve the real problem, don't treat the symptom. Spread the good news. Let others know when they have done a good job. And lastly, always wear a smiling face and have fun.

PART II
LEADERSHIP AND STYLES

"Nothing would get done at all if a man waited until he could do something so well that no one could find fault with it"

-- John Henry Cardinal Newman

CHAPTER TWO

EFFECTIVE MANAGEMENT APPROACH

"The best executive is the one who has sense enough to pick good men to do what he wants done, and self-restraint enough to keep from meddling with them while they do it"
                                                        --Theodore Roosevelt

"The highest reward for a person's toil is not what they get for it, but what they become by it."
                                                        -- Anonymous

Leadership is not management. Management is a bottom line focus: How can I best accomplish certain things? Leadership deals with the top line: What are the things I want to accomplish? In the words of both Peter Drucker and Warren Bennis, "Management is doing things right; leadership is doing the right things." Management is efficiency in climbing the ladder of success; leadership determines whether the ladder is leaning against the right wall. (Covey, 1990, p. 101).

Effective leader come in all shapes and sizes; the only thing they have in common is the ability to get things done. (Drucker 1998). An effective leader must find the right balance between managing a business, managing work and workers and managing the organization or the institution in the community and society.

The essence of managing business lies in using resources in a manner that adds value as perceived by the institution's key stakeholders. When a value is added, an institution produces a far greater good for the consumers, for the employees, and for the society at large.

Managing work and workers is one of the essential functions of management hence he or she makes work very productive. In order to make work productive, managers must first understand what work needs to be done and how to organize it. To deliver services effectively, organizing work and workers into functional departments and positions is a necessary step. When this task is achieved, the next step in achieving productivity is building a cooperative spirit among the workers through leadership and motivation.

The challenge for the effective leadership lies in creating a workplace environment in which each staff contributes his or her best efforts toward goals that are important to management. The effective leader understands that if work and workers are mismanaged, organizational performance will suffer no matter how good the manager may be in managing the business side of the operation. (Drucker 1998). Creating values for employees - such as rewarding them in the form of wages, benefits, personal satisfaction, self-esteem and individual development - is a must if an organization wants to increase productivity.

It is important for the leadership of an organization to constantly evaluate whether the institution is making positive strides in connecting with the community and whether it is adequately discharging its responsibility toward society and community.

In business, the market is changing so rapidly that many products and services that successfully met consumer tastes and needs a few years ago are obsolete today. Proactive powerful leadership must constantly monitor environmental change, particularly customer buying habits and motives, and provide the force necessary to organize resources in the right direction.

Such changes as deregulation of the airline industry, skyrocketing costs of health care, and the greater quality and quantity of imported cars impact the environment in significant ways. If industries do not monitor the environment, including their own work teams, and exercise the creative leadership to keep headed in the right direction, no amount of management expertise can keep them from failing.

Efficient management without effective leadership is, as one individual has phrased it, "like straightening deck chairs on the Titanic," No management success can compensate for failure in leadership. But leadership is hard because we're often caught in a management paradigm.

An effective leader of any organization is a person capable of organizing the resources and finances available to best meet the needs of the customers. In successfully accomplishing this, the leadership makes innumerable decisions.

Management involves decision making. What the administrator does for the hospital or nursing facility is make decisions about what ought to happen in that facility. Although there is extensive literature describing the field of management theory, many authors have returned again and again to a basic set of activities as the best explanation of what managers do.

Luther Gulick, an early 20th century author, defined the manager's tasks as:

Planning, Organizing, Staffing, Directing, Coordinating, Reporting, Forecasting, and Budgeting (Gulick & Lyndall, 1937, p. 13).

Several decades later Earnest Dale, in his textbook, *Management Theory and Practice*, differed only slightly in his description. He agreed on the importance of the first tasks, but consolidated the last four under three rubrics: controlling, innovating, and representing (1969, pp. 5-7).

A manager is involved in directing, staffing organizing, planning, forecasting, budgeting, directing, evaluating, controlling, innovating, and marketing? Let's look at each one of them briefly.

Directing is the process of providing direction (preliminary training and ongoing supervision) through communication to each employee who thereby learns what is expected of him or her.

Staffing is hiring the right persons for each well-defined job in the organization. It is one of the most difficult tasks the administrator and department managers face because it is seldom possible to predict from an interview and recommendations how a person will work out on the job

Organizing is deciding how to structure a suitable organization to implement the plan, put it into action. This will include the number of people needed for the staff and the materials with which to build or to work.

Planning is deciding what needs to be done and makes a set of plans to accomplish it.

Forecasting is projecting trends and needs which the facility management must meet in the future.

Budgeting is projecting costs and establishing categories with dollar amounts for each

Evaluating is judging or comparing the extent to which the organization is accomplishing its actual to expected goals.

Controlling Quality is taking steps to assure that the goals are accomplished and that each job is done as planned.

Innovating is leading the staff to develop new ideas that enable the facility to enhance its attractiveness to the community served.

Marketing is assuring that the facility successfully attracts and admits the persons it seeks to serve.

These are some basic functions of a highly effective leader, or a manager. The reader may wish to use other words and concepts to describe these functions, or even improve on the model. Certainly a leader does much more than has been described above (Pressman & Wildavsky, 1974). However, if forecasting, planning, organizing, staffing, directing, evaluating, controlling, innovating, and marketing are not successfully accomplished, the minimum leadership responsibilities of an organization have not been fulfilled.

In his book, *A Passion for Excellence*, Tom Peters (1985) advocates a simple four-part scheme of management's role: care of customers, constant innovation, turned-on people, and leadership. He observes that in both the for-profit and not-for-profit sectors, superior performance, over the long haul, depends on two things: (a) taking exceptional care of clients (customers) via superior service and superior quality of care and (b) constant innovation.

He observes that financial control is vital, but that one does not sell financial control, but rather a quality service or product (excellently cared for customers). A hospital or nursing home facility seldom sustains superior performance merely by having all the beds full; superior is sustained through innovation in ways to serve residents/patients/customers and promote market development. Efficient management of the budget is vital in an organization such as a university or a factory, he observes, yet a great university is never characterized by the remark, "It has a good budget" (Peters, 1985, p.4). Just as the superb university is superb only by virtue of its success in serving its ultimate customer, the students, the superb hospital or nursing home is superb only by virtue of its success in serving its ultimate customers, the patients and their families or significant others.

Peters (1985, p.3) advocates a management model based on what he calls " a blinding flash of the obvious." Giving every employee the space to innovate, at least a little. Answering the hones and resident call buttons with common courtesy. Doing things that work (giving quality care). Listening to customers and stake holders and asking them for their ideas, then acting on them. Soliciting input from staff, and implement them as appropriate.

Nancy R. Hellyer, (President and CEO, Saint Joseph Regional Medical Center, 2006) embarking on $355 million facility, wrote in 2006 to the patients of Saint Joseph's and members of the greater St. Joseph County community that for more than a century, the founders and leaders of Saint Joseph Regional Medical Center (SJRMC) and its predecessor organizations have embraced the opportunity to serve the healthcare needs of the greater South Bend, IN region. She continues by saying that "To continue delivering our unique blend of faith-based compassion and outstanding care to our patients, the SJRMC Board of Trustees, our Associates, leadership, physicians and I have embarked on an ambitious plan to construct a progressive, forward-looking new facility."

Leadership Defined

It would be useful to examine various definitions of leadership, what it involves, and what different interpretations of leadership reveal. A comparison of Christian leadership with industrial leadership and the effects of such leadership in industry would show how Christian leaders may learn from industry.

Clarence A. Weber (Weber, 1961), says that leadership is a moral function best known by the personalities it enriches and not necessarily by the smoothness of operation or the number of persons it captivates. Furthermore, Weber feels that leadership is a process to help people examine, evaluate, change, and develop roles and purposes. Whenever a group feels the need to assess its basic values, leadership is needed to make three specific kinds of judgments:

1. Judgments concerning fundamental principles which should govern subsequent decision making.

2. Judgments concerning formulation of policies which are consistent with principles.

3. Judgments concerning specific decisions which are consistent with policies adopted and with basic principles to which the group has made commitment.

Weber suggests that an administrator who is dissatisfied with operations simply because they are governed by mere habit rather than by commitment to basic principles exhibits true leadership qualities.

P.J.W. Pigors defines leadership as "the process of mutual stimulation which controls human energy in the pursuit of common cause." (Pigors, 1935). C. A. Gible says that leadership is the quality of a status official's performance within a group and at the same time refers to the quality of the structure of the group. (Gible, 1947). However, John K. Hemphill claims that "leadership is the behavior of an individual who is involved in directing group activities." (Hemphill, 1949). In this one short sentence he sums up the basic definition of all leadership-the directing of group activities. Yet, how an individual directs these activities, in what spirit-humane or bureaucratic-will determine the ultimate success or failure of those group activities.

Ordway Tead defines leadership as "the process of helping a group to achieve goals which seem desirable to the group." (Tead, 1935). It is interesting to note that Tead stresses the obvious importance of "helping" as against Hemphill who uses the word "directing"-an informative and significant distinction which differentiates considerably between the humane and the bureaucratic approach.

Control by "agreement" is naturally more democratic than "directing" control. The more democratic control inspires others to assume individual responsibility. Such leadership provides opportunity for all to work, learn, and grow together. Education in its semantic connotation means the "drawing out" (Latin, *educere*) and democratic leadership draws out ides and inspires others to act on initiative within an atmosphere of mutual cooperation.

Democratic control involves open participation, a sharing in planning and evaluation at all levels. Democratic control should guarantee that each member of the group is given opportunity to make his/her own contribution. Democratic control should help to resolve any conflicts through mutual discussion rather than authoritarian pronouncements.

Some individuals in a position of authority hesitate to share decision making; whereas, democratic control governs by majority rule while protecting the minority rights. Ellen G. White spoke about the obstinate man:

"Obstinacy is a barrier to all improvement... He (an obstinate man) may have abundant reason to see that he is wrong; his brethren may raise their voices against his opinions and his methods for making a success of the work; but he cherishes an almost immovable bar against conviction." "Such a man," she continued, "should not be placed on boards or committees. He is constitutionally unfitted to make decisions." (White, 1898).

Evidently such a person cannot be used in democratic decision making wherein cooperation is essential. Ellen White emphatically stated,

"Let no one man feel that his gift alone is sufficient for the work of God....In order for the work to be built up strong and symmetrical, there is need of varied gifts and different agencies, of thinking that his talent is sufficient to make a complete whole." (White, 1898).

The servant of the Lord directs God's church to follow democratic principles of decision making. Problems, therefore, can be resolved by the majority rather than by the individual. The group can use a much wider range of resources and experience than one individual could provide. Such democracy would inspire increasing freedom and authoritarian methods would disappear.

Leadership and Organization

Organizations that thrive over an extended period of time (years) depend on *effective leaders*-persons who have foresight combined with an ability to guide the organization to successfully take advantage of the opportunities the future offers.

Management is the art of managing process or day-to-day activities of an organization while leading or leadership is the art of managing managers or people.

Just as a satisfactory description of "deciding" is elusive, so is leading. There are, however, those who propose the "leadership theory," suggesting that history is made or measurably influenced by individuals who become leaders. Whatever one might think of their accomplishments, persons such as Alexander the Great, Genghis Kahn, Confucius, Joan of Arc, George Washington, Abraham Lincoln, Margaret Sanger, Winston Churchill seem to have assumed leadership roles that affected the course of history.

Leadership in the business world seems to be no less crucial to the success of organizations. Between the years 1915 and 1973 Thomas Watson, Sr., and Thomas Watson Jr., provided leadership to an organization, International Business Machines Corporation (IBM), that came to dominate the computer world only during their tenure-because this father and son had foresight (successfully predicted the future) combined with an ability to guide the organization (IBM) to successfully take advantage of the opportunities offered by the future. It was not until being discharged from a job he had held for 14 years that Tom Watson,

Sr., joined a company that manufactured scales, meat slicers, time clocks, and punch cards for data sorting. He envisioned that these punch cards could revolutionize the future. He borrowed money and renamed the company. At the time, 1924, his son commented, "What a big name for a pipsqueak company that makes meat grinders" (Kriegel, 1991, p. 39). International Business Machines Corporation had just been born.

When IBM's leadership changed after 60 years under the Watsons the giant lost its leadership position. The company had ridden the wave of change for 60 years with them at the helm. When the Watsons led IBM it usually was ranked in *Fortune Magazine's* annual survey of America's Most Admired Corporations as #1. Lou Gertsner, IBM president in the mid-1990s, stated several times that he did not have to have a vision to lead the corporation. By 1995, out of the 500 ranked companies, IBM had dropped from the most admired corporation to the 281st most admired corporation! Leadership counts. The Watsons inspired IBM to six decades of greatness with a vision. Vision, it seems, also counts ("America's Most Admired Corporations," 1995; Hamel & Prahalad, 1994).

In the world of automobile manufacturing there is a general agreement that Lee Iacocca's abilities changed the American auto industry in the mid-60s by creating the Mustang, a car that sold an unbelievable 418,812 in its first year alone. He championed the miraculous rebirth of Chrysler Corporation from near bankruptcy to repayment of its controversial $1.2 billion loan so early that Washington didn't even know how to cash the check and he brought Chrysler into a position of leadership in the industry. (Iacocca, 1984, p.280).

Leadership therefore can be defined as influencing people to act for certain goals that represent the values and motivations such as wants, needs, aspirations, and expectations of both leaders and followers. (Burns 1998). Northouse (2001) concluded that leadership is a process that requires continuity and involves give and take between the leader and the followers. Leadership affects the followers and its essence is to influence the followers. Leadership occurs within a group or "people" context and its meaning is found in relation to other people because the need for leadership dissipates when there are no people to be led. Leadership involves goal attainment by directing their energies toward individuals who are trying to achieve something together.

Conflict Management

There is probably no aspect of leadership more important than the ability to manage a conflict. When conflicts arise, as they always will, leaders must stay focused on the main task at hand. You can't allow yourself to get distracted by side issues. You must project calm in the face of the crisis, so your staff will be calm, too. That way you'll get valuable input and feedback from your subordinate. And once you've come to a decision on how to handle the crisis, you must be firm and confident in your course of action.

Conflict is unpleasant and sometimes dysfunctional but it is an unavoidable aspect of any organization.

1. *Don't ignore a crisis.* Crises are inevitable and they don't just go away. You must learn how to manage them. In the mid-1990s, a Web site popped up that parodied the Muppet Bert from *Sesame Street*. It was called "Bert Is Evil and had doctored photographs showing Bert with Adolf Hitler, the KKK, and Osama bin Laden. At the time, the Sesame Workshop (the producer of television's *Sesame Street*) didn't do much to fight these images; then, in 2001, after the attacks of September 11, the image of Bert with Osama was used in anti-American posters at a violent protest in Bangladesh. Naturally, this was picked up by the media and widely publicized. Had Sesame Workshop fought to have the pictures removed from the Web site earlier, it could have avoided this negative exposure. Now, the company has a plan to fight such abuse and more actively protects its image. If the *Sesame Street* producers had taken decisive action at the time, they not only would have discouraged other offenders, but would have had a legal basis to demonstrate that such misuse is commercially damaging for them. Don't ignore a crisis. Develop a plan to attack it an prevent it from happening again.

2. *Learn to make educated decisions.* The advice you receive is likely to be divided; consensus in crisis situations is rare, so don't wait for it. The bigger the decision, the less likely you are to get everyone to agree. The U.S. president has the power to mobilize troops in a national crisis. To wait for consensus in Congress might be too

late to handle an immediate threat. Weigh the pros and cons of each choice and make an educated decision. That's why you are the leader.

3. *Don't be rattle or swayed by new development.* Don't allow unexpected developments to divert you from your main course unless there is good reason. Outside events can occur because of stupidity or carelessness as easily as by design. Make sure you thoroughly evaluate "evidence" before making any decisions.

4. *Keep your cool.* If you show indecision or fear, that will inevitably communicate itself to those you are trying to lead. One of today's best-know leaders, former New York Mayor Rudolph Giuliani, makes a point of saying that the key to crisis management is to get calmer as the situation escalates. That way you can think clearly and make better decisions than if you let yourself become distracted. In addition, it is hoped that those around you will follow your lead.

Learning From Mistakes

It's often said that we learn much more from our mistakes than we ever do from our successes. All leaders make mistakes; you can't avoid them. However, you can look at your mistakes, figure out where you went wrong, and try to avoid making the same mistake in the future. Leaders also have to be ale to admit when they have made a mistake. They can't foist responsibility off on someone else. If you do this, you'll soon find resentment and a lack of respect growing among your subordinates and peers.

1. *Admit failures.* Mistakes and misjudgments are unavoidable; what counts is how you react to them. Many leaders don't want to lose face by admitting failures. But sometimes the admission is a necessary first step to addressing an issue. Kennedy's acknowledgement of his personal responsibility for the Bay of Pigs fiasco and Clinton's admission to Monica's affair kept the political fallout to a minimum.

2. *Right the mistake*, and avoid similar ones. Don't focus on the fact that you made a mistake. Try instead to focus on avoiding similar mistakes and rectifying the one you made. Kennedy's turnaround on civil rights was heralded by his June 11, 1963, speech to the nation. He didn't dwell on the mistakes of the past or his own misreading of the situation. As their leader, he called upon Americans to follow him in righting a longtime wrong.

3. *Remain objective*. Don't let recovering from a setback become a personal vendetta; when things get personal, they get ugly. You should have to maintain enough distance to be objective and make the right decision. Kennedy allowed his intense dislike of Castro to cloud his judgment in relation to Cuba and its head of state. However, he recognized a certain kinship between himself and Khrushchev despite their strong differences of opinion. This helped him to defuse the Cuban missile crisis by giving the Russian leader a bit of leeway rather than backing him into a corner.

4. *Avoid tunnel vision.* What you think is most important may not in fact be what is most important. To avoid tunnel vision, you should make sure you do enough research into what the problem is. Check with all parties concerned. Get good advisers, and include opinions from people who have handled different situations. By continually checking your opinions against those around you, you can determine whether you are addressing the right issue in the right way. Many successful companies use 360-degree feedback for their leaders. This review process allows people in all positions -- those working under the leader, on par with the leader, and above the leader in the hierarchy -- to give the top executive feedback. It is a quick and effective way to determine whether you are meeting the needs of your organization.

Principles of Management

An effective leader utilizes different approaches when dealing with power, authority, rewards and incentives. Here are some examples of how they should be used.

Using Authority
1. Make polite requests, not arrogant demands.
2. Make requests in clear, simple language; check for staff understanding
3. Explain reasons for requests
4. Follow up to check for compliance.

Using Rewards
1. Don't overemphasize incentives; staff will expect rewards for every request. Emphasize mutual loyalty and teamwork.
2. Rewards are unlikely to produce commitment.
3. Reinforce past behavior; don't bribe for future performance.
4. The size of rewards should reflect total performance.
5. Money is not the only (and is often the least effective) reward.
6. Avoid appearing manipulative at all costs.

Using Coercive Power
1. Avoid coercion and punishment except when absolutely necessary.
2. Punish only to deter extremely detrimental behavior
3. Try to determine genuine fault before criticizing.
4. Discipline promptly and consistently without favoritism. Fit the punishment to the seriousness of the infarction.
5. State warnings without hostility; remain calm and express desire to help subordinate comply with requirements and avoid punishment.
6. Invite subordinate to share in responsibility for correcting disciplinary problems; set improvement goals and develop improvement plans.
7. Warn before punishing; don't issue idle or exaggerated warnings you are not prepared to carry out.

Using Expert Power
1. Preserve credibility by avoiding careless statements and rash decisions.
2. Keep informed about technical developments affecting the group's work.

3. In a crisis, remain calm; act confidently and decisively.
4. Avoid arrogance or "talking down" to staff; show respect for staff ideas and suggestions and incorporate them whenever feasible.
5. Do not threaten subordinates' self-esteem.
6. Recognize subordinates' concerns; explain why a proposed plan of action is best and, what steps will be taken to minimize risk to them.

Using Referent Power
1. Be considerate, show concern for staff needs and feelings, treat them fairly, and defend their interests to superiors and outsiders.
2. Avoid expressing hostility, distrust, rejection, or indifference toward subordinates. Actions speak louder than words.
3. Explain the personal importance of requests and your reliance on staff support and cooperation.
4. Don't make requests too often; make requests reasonable.
5. Be a good role model.

Adapted from G.A. Yukl and Taber, "The Effective Use of Managerial Power," *Personnel* (March-April 1983).

CHAPTER THREE

DEVELOPMENT OF LEADERSHIP THEORIES

A great leader never sets himself above his followers
except in carrying responsibilities

--Jules Ormont

Of the best leaders, the people only know they exist;
The next best they love and praise; the next they fear; and
the next they revile.
When they do not command the people's faith; some lose
faith in them,
And they resort to recriminations!
But of the best, when their task is accomplished, their work
done,
The people all remark, "We have done it ourselves."

Lao-Tze (c. 600 B.C.)

The history of mankind provides ample proof of the multiple effects of leadership upon those who are led, with or without their consent. Consider the effect of leaders such as Genghis Khan, who spread his power across Asia to the borders of Europe; of Napoleon, whose conquests spread across Europe; of Hitler, whose conquests and authoritarian leadership eventually led to the death of millions.

According to C.H. Titus, leadership is "the art of getting what one wants and making the people like it." (Titus, 1950). This is similar to Hitler' concept of leadership. Arthur Bloomberg (Blumberg, 1959) suggests that autocratic leadership and insecurity are positively correlated. Those who are committed to the principles of democracy must assess Titus' definition as contrary to their conceptions of leadership.

There must be something further to leadership. This is, of course, the leadership of ideas. Ideas can inspire. Books therefore can inspire, but it is the person who can lead. Some persons, inspired by ideas, can transmit those ideas in practical terms to others and, consequently, inspire others to follow. The result is either a great benefit or detriment to humanity. Hitler conceived the book *Mein Kampf* which, backed up his inspiring and forceful personality, resulted in Nazism. But such characters often led forcibly or by the sheer strength of their outgoing personalities. This however, is not true leadership in the strictest sense. True leadership must lead, not dominate. It must inspire and encourage, not force and bully. True leadership must arouse in others an emergent leadership. It must inspire in others the wish to lead however dormant or latent their leadership ability may be.

Theories Of Leadership

The study of leadership theory deals with an explanation of leadership phenomena. There are four main theories on leadership: trait theory, situational theory, follower ship theory, and eclectic theory. (Johnson, et al., 1970).

Trait theory. The trait theory holds that leaders are successful because they possess certain traits such as forcefulness, intelligence, thoughtfulness, fairness, and so on. It is difficult to establish whether traits have direct bearing on success as a leader or if a surplus of one trait can compensate for a shortage of another. In spite of the limitations of the theory, Ernest Dale (Dale, 1978) suggests that traits are frequently used to select leaders and followers in management. Probably this exists in educational fields also.

Situational Theory. The situational theory claims that the individual best suited for leadership will arise from within the group. The leader will have a distinct advantage and will have demonstrated his/her ability when he/she assumes a formal leadership position. The formal followers, however, may reject his/her leadership as conditions change. Hence, for such leaders, success is not guaranteed. The choice of the leader will depend upon the problem and the character of the group itself.

Followership Theory. Follower ship theory, a modification of the trait theory, assumes that the best indicator of the quality of a leader is the quality of his/her followers. Consequently, the best way to evaluate the leader is to analyze the followers, and good leadership is the ability to build self-starting and self-reliant followers. Poor leadership would be indicated if followers are overly dependent.

Eclectic Theory. Eclectic theory uses information from all the other theories. As more information on leadership becomes available and is analyzed, the leader, rather than depending only on his/her intuition, makes use of such knowledge in decision making. Eclectic theory is, perhaps, the most useful because it provides for expansion and combines the best features of all theories in making dynamic leadership. Leadership theories, like any part of administration, must change to meet the demand of time and place.

McGregor's Theory X and Theory Y.

Perhaps no other person provided a more unique knowledge on leadership theories than did Douglas McGregor. (McGregory, 1960). He provided the traditional view of direction and control. Then he provided the assumption of theory Y, the integration of individual and organizational goals. First, let us look at the concepts of Theory X. Three assumptions of Theory X, the traditional view of directional and control follow.

1. The average human being has an inherent dislike for work and will avoid it if he can

2. Because of this dislike for work, most people must be coerced, controlled, directed, or threatened to get them to strive for the achievement of organizational objectives.

3. The average human being prefers to be directed, wishes to avoid all responsibility, has little ambition, and wants security above all.

With these concepts in mind, let us now consider the assumptions of Theory Y, the integration of individual and organizational goals:

1. Expenditure of physical and mental effort in work is as natural as play or rest.
2. External control and threats are not the only means for bringing about effort toward organizational objectives. Man will exercise self-direction toward objectives to which he is committed.
3. Commitment to objectives is a function of the rewards associated with achievement.
4. Under proper conditions, the average human being learns to accept and seek responsibility.
5. The capacity to exercise a relatively high degree of creativity in the solution of organizational problems is widely distributed in the population.
6. Under the conditions of modern industrial life, the intellectual potential of the average person is only partially utilized.

Both theories assume that management is responsible for organizing the elements of productive enterprise. The elements may be money, materials, equipment, people, and so on. McGregor's ideas have some wide applications to all kinds of organizations. It appears that Theory X has a tendency toward authoritarian, autocratic, and totalitarian administration, whereas the concepts of Theory Y has a democratic formulation. Some strides have been made toward Theory Y, but attitudes of the establishment-constituents, administrators, and workers alike-will have to change.

Theory Z (The Process of Change)

Dr. William G. Ouchi, a professor in the Graduate School of Management at the University California in Los Angeles, is the propounder of Theory Z. He began to study Japanese business-management practices in the early 1970s and finished his book on Theory Z. He began to study Japanese business-management practices in the early 1970s and finished his book on Theory Z in the 1980s. He found that the secret to Japanese success is not technology but a special way of managing people. According to Theory Z, a management style focuses on a strong company philosophy, a distinct corporate culture, long-range staff development, and consensus decision making.

Dr. Ouchi believes that an organization consists not only of the corporation but of its suppliers, customers, and community. Consequently, no one could change a whole organization all at once. However, Dr. Ouchi suggested a series of steps for the process of transformation from a type A Company to a type Z Company. This series of steps is often overlapping and its sequence is often changing. Although the development process is slow, it is worth trying. The process, as Dr. Ouchi described it, has the objective of developing the ability of the organization to coordinate people to achieve productivity. It is not based on technology. In other words, people's work attitude and commitment to their jobs must be improved first. The following points should be of interest to students of theory:

1. *Understand the Type Z organization and your role.* Understanding involves learning what type Z organization is all about and what is the role of people in the organization. Understanding could be accomplished through reading, discussion, and making a start. Understanding comes from the open expression of skepticism through a process of debate and of analysis; thus it is important to present the reading and the ideas in a manner that invites an open display of skepticism. The development of trust is one way to invite skepticism to accept Theory Z. Trust consists of understanding that people share fundamentally compatible goals in the long run, and thus they have reason to trust one another. People in the organization must create a desire for a more effective working relationship together and that no one desires to harm others. Both complete openness and candor in a relationship are needed in developing trust. Once understanding and trust are developed, cooperation will follow.

2. *Auditing the company's philosophy.* A company's philosophy helps to suggest the ways in which the people should behave in the organization and the way the organization is to behave in response to its people, its clients, and the community it serves. A company's philosophy sets forth the company's motivating spirit for all to understand; it also determines how insiders and outsiders alike appraise, trust, and value the company and its products. In order to develop a philosophy, it is necessary first to understand the company's culture and to know the direction of the company and how it uses consistencies over time. Analyzing four or five key decisions the company has made in the past will help one to find the company's culture. Auditing the company's philosophy and objectives must be done early in the time sequence.

3. *Define the desired management philosophy and involve the company leader.* In other words, one must set out the desired philosophy. The organizational leader must be involved directly in this step. Ultimately, a process of organizational change cannot succeed without the direct and personal support of the top person in the hierarchy. The top manager has as incentive to develop, over time, a trusting relationship that permits sharing of the decision-making authority with subordinates. Failure to transfer the ideas can occur if the leader fails to speak out and is not included in the consensus decision regarding preparation.

4. *Implement the philosophy by creating both structures and incentives.* Most organizations need structure to guide them subtlety towards cooperation and long view. It is important that each person in the organization understands so well his/her task and its relationship to other tasks that the coordination is unspoken. Teamwork is essential. Well-organized structures give way to trust, openness, and habitual use of teamwork.

5. *Develop interpersonal skills.* Two types of skills should be developed: (a) The first is to recognize patterns of interaction in the decision-making and problem-solving groups. One way to develop them is

to try role playing outside the context of a formal meeting. Another possibility is the fish-bowl exercise. In this, one group observes behavior, takes notes, and then feeds back to the discussants their observations of who led, in what style, who interrupted, who contributed little, and so on. (b) The second is to learn to provide leadership in such a group. This involves enhancing efficiency and speed or working.

6. *Test yourself and the system.* A self test need not be elaborate nor expensive, but it must be capable of helping to convince the skeptic that a person's concerns were unfounded. The following points were mentioned: (a) When going well, the manager's lot becomes less hurried but also less pleasing. Less selfish pleasure results in not so much flattery as in a type A organization. (b) There should be less comfort, less sense of power, more questioning of decisions.

7. *Involve the union.* A Type Z company has to involve the union in its plans. Dealing with the union is among the most emotionally charged elements in a process of organizational development. Since the Type Z organization relies to a great extent upon an egalitarian distribution of power for its success, one way to achieve this is through the creation of workers' councils or a union. However, in Type Z organizations, trust lessens dependence on restrictive protection so the unions feel threatened.

8. *Stabilize employment.* One way to stabilize employment is to provide employees with a work environment that offers equity, challenge, and participation in decisions about their work. The cost to the firm of layoffs shows up in greater difficulty in hiring the most talented employees in the future, in the higher cost of voluntary turnover, and in the lower commitment of the employees who stay. Other methods should be used to stave off financial problems rather than laying off employees. They provide a better way to stabilize employment.

9. *Decide on a system for slow evaluation and promotion.* Slowing down the process of evaluation and promotion is vital to underscore to

employees the importance of long-run performance. The approach overlooks the fact that the best people always have the most outside options and that impatient young people may irrationally leave a more promising career with a Type Z company to join a Type A company. However, the solution to the problem is to promote newer employees rapidly, compared to the competition, so that they will not leave, but promote them slowly, compared to their peers, so that they will develop a long-run view.

10. *Broaden career path development.* According to Theory Z, it is believed that managers who continue to circulate across jobs within a company, but without hierarchical promotion, retain their enthusiasm, their effectiveness, and their satisfaction at a level almost as high as that of the ones who continue to move both around and up. In other words, widening career paths is accepted in Theory Z type organizations. Circulating staff through departments, including management, is approved. This may even mean a drop in the individual's level of management for a time.

11. *Preparing for implementation at the first level.* All the stages of implementation to this point have focused on managerial and professional employees. Changing at the first level after higher levels have been achieved is important since lower level employees or managers cannot participate unless those above provide the invitation to do so. The lower-level will overcome the deepest sort of skepticism through great effort and only with the most consistent signals from the first and higher level. In a bureaucracy, rigid hierarchies only permit evolutionary change to start at the top. Change at the bottom is always revolutionary.

12. *Seek out areas to implement participation.* It is believed that significant gains in productivity have been achieved by companies through the application of participative approaches at the office or shop-floor level. Therefore, real participation must be implemented especially in the floor level, not the question-box; involvement, if necessary, must be during company time. Conferences, study groups, planning

sessions, and workers' ideas must be implemented wherever possible.

13. *Permit the development of holistic relationships.* A holistic relationship cannot be developed until Z Theory changes are underway. Then it has a chance to grow. Thus, opportunity must be given for the development of holistic relationships. Employee's feeling of belonging is the kind of atmosphere needed in a Type Z organization. The development on overt occasions. Hence, work-related issues hold the key to holistic relations and keep them free of any company paternalism.

Steps 1 to 10 of the Process of Change may take up to two years before the first level is affected, and this change can only be accomplished through the influence of trust and consistency. The whole process of transfer can take from 10 to 15 years if every worker is to be involved.

CHAPTER FOUR

EFFECTIVE LEADERSHIP STYLES

"Leadership is about looking for the good in others, then you discover the best in yourself. It is about not following where the path may lead. Go instead where there is no path and leave a trait."

--Anonymous

The search for effective leadership characteristics as personality traits or personal attributes has not been productive. For every example of a great leader with certain characteristics, ten examples of leadership failure on the part of individuals processing those same characteristics can easily be found. By the early 1950s, it had become clear that the situation itself is a major determinant of the extent to which leadership characteristics have any influence at all in determining leadership effectiveness (Stogdill, 1974).

At about this same time, several researchers began to focus more on what leaders do rather than on what personal characteristics they possess. Thus, leadership behavior research in laboratories at Harvard University found "activity," "task ability," and "likeability" leadership behaviors. Studies at Ohio State University were conducted in field settings where subordinates were asked to describe the behaviors exhibited by their leaders. Two major dimensions were identified from the behaviors, one called "consideration" and the other, "initiating structure." Researchers at the University of Michigan also conducted research in the field but asked leaders themselves to describe what they did. This effort produced two major dimensions of leadership behavior: "job-centered behavior" and "employee-centered behavior." (Sullivan et all. 1992).

Similarities across these research efforts are remarkably consistent. In each case, concern for the task was identified as a major aspect of leadership behavior (task ability, initiating structure, job-centered behavior), as was a second major dimension dealing with interpersonal relationships (likeability, consideration, employee-centered behavior).

Specifically, *initiating structure* refers to behavior in which the nurse manager organizes and defines the work to be accomplished and establishes well-defined, routine work patterns, channels of communication, and methods of getting the job done. For example, management provides a detailed manual of job descriptions, personnel policies, and procedures for requesting time off on certain holidays. *Consideration,* on the other hand, refers to behavior that conveys mutual trust, respect, friendship, warmth, and rapport between the nurse manager and staff members. In this situation, the employee learns to expect that the nurse manager will hear a complaint openly without any reprisal.

Focusing on manager behaviors to improve staff performance is supported by Jenkins and Henderson (1984), who examined how staff nurse, who perform the bulk of patient care, perceived the behaviors of charge nurses. Nurse manager behaviors that recognized the staff nurse's need for belonging, love, social activity, self-respect, status within the organization were viewed as essential for motivation as well as for quality patient care.

In general, the consistency of research on leader behavior has been encouraging, but the relationship of leader behaviors to leader effectiveness has proved to be puzzling. Neither increases in task behavior nor interpersonal behavior necessarily increased leadership effectiveness or employee job performance. Nevertheless, this earlier focus on leadership behavior has been a significant advance in understanding leadership effectiveness. The search for leadership styles or clusters of leadership behaviors began in an attempt to identify particular patterns or styles of leadership that would be most effective in most situations.

Choosing To Lead

Deciding on one's approach to lead is one of the more important decisions managers ever make. Kriegel (1991), compares leading an organization to riding the waves of change. The time to change is when you don't have to, he asserts, when you are on the crest of a wave, not when you are in the trough. In the world of health care delivery administration the surf is up! Waves of change are coming from government, third-party payers, and the patients/customers and their families. The best surfers (administrators/leaders) are not necessarily the best swimmers (best management theoreticians).

As Kriegel (1991), has suggested, the future is coming at us like enormous waves of change in set after set, and the waves are getting bigger. The surf is up in the hospital industry, the home health care industry, and the managed care industry. The future belongs to those who decide to ride, to those who welcome the unexpected.

John F.Welch, as president of General Electric, became widely regarded as the leading master of corporate change through shedding 200,000 employees while tripling GE's market value between 1981 and 1993. He believes that every business must be fast and adaptable to survive. People ask, he observes, Is the change over (at GE)? Can we stop now? He responds that change has just begun, that it is never ending. Change, he asserts, is a continuing process, not an event. He sees the administrator's job as listening to, searching for, and spreading ideas-the process of exposing people to good ideas and role models (Welch, 1993).

Leadership Styles and Personality

With the realization that different combinations of leader behaviors might produce different effects, some researchers began studying ways in which successful leadership is accomplished, or how leaders delegate tasks and how they communicate with their staff members. Thus, leadership styles are clusters of behaviors that characterize the manner in which a manager uses interpersonal behaviors to influence the accomplishment of unit goals and the kinds of social power used. While the number of "leadership styles" one can find in the management literature almost rivals the number of personality traits once thought to be critical to leadership effectiveness, five general styles of leadership have frequently been identified.

Many studies have shown that leadership styles include what a leader does, says, and how he/she acts. It is the study of a leader's approach to the use of authority and participation in decision making. These typical leadership styles and their effects are outlined below.

1. *Authoritarian or autocratic style.*

The authoritarian or autocratic leader is primarily concerned with task accomplishment rather than relationships. Primarily uses directive leadership behaviors. Tends to make decisions alone. Expects respect and obedience of staff. Frequently exercises power with coercion. Useful and necessary in crisis situations.

The authoritarian or autocratic leader derives vested authority through the office more than from personal attributes. He/she seeks very little group participation in decision making. The follower becomes dependent on the leader, finding security in the fact that he/she knows exactly what is required of him/her. The follower's personal development, however, is sacrificed. If the leader should leave, subordinates are generally not prepared for promotion. (Marks, Stoops, & King-Stoops, 1971).

2. *Laissez-faire or permissive style.*

Complete permissiveness is allowed in the laissez-faire or permissive style of leadership. The group lacks direction because the leader does not help in making decisions. He/she merely supplies various materials or contributes when asked. The group is given too much responsibility to proceed in any direction. Tends to have few established goals or policies; abstains from leading. Not generally useful in highly structured organizations (e.g., health care institutions). If this style functions for a long period of time, it may easily develop into anarchy. (Kast & Rosenzweig, 1985).

3. Bureaucratic style

The bureaucratic style of leadership is based on a system of files to solve all problems. It is too well organized. Many present-day complex organizations are bureaucratic. Insecure leader finds security in following established policies. Power is exercised by fixed, relatively inflexible rules. Leader tends to relate impersonally to staff. He or she avoids decision making without standards or norms for guidance.

The leader is saddled with looking after routine activities with guidelines established by the system itself. This tends to depersonalize the organization. Robert Goldhammer, in discussing teachers, states, "While bureaucratic supervision (by directive, by fiat, by form and by rate) may satisfy administrative priorities on efficiency, it simply does not speak to the critical questions of progressional existence that determine each teacher's functioning individually." (Goldhammer, 1980).

4. Charismatic style.

"Charisma" is a word so frequently associated with John F. Kennedy that it actually began to grate on his successor. "I may not have charisma," Lyndon B. Johnson growled to an aid, "but I got the bills passed." (Barnes et al., 2005, p. 50).

Many successful leaders have gotten by on little or no charisma. Nevertheless, charisma remains a potentially powerful leadership tool. Lee Iacocca, generally considered one of the most charismatic business leaders of recent years, made masterful use of his powerful public personality to convince a highly reluctant Congress and a skeptical public to go along with a publicly financed bailout of the ailing Chrysler.

New York Times columnist William Safire, in his *New Political Dictionary*, describes charisma (which is rooted in the Greek word *charism*, or "gift") as "political sex appeal." It is a certain magnetism and charm that draws others to you. It is, to some extent, a bit of a confidence trick played on those around you. People will not follow an individual in whom they repose little confidence. Charisma can help generate that confidence. To be described as a charismatic leader is almost always a compliment; to be described as "charisma challenged" definitely is not.

It is advisable to note that charisma can be used for evil as well as good. Many of Adolf Hitler's comrades in the trenches of the First World War, or those who knew him as a failed artist in Vienna, were later flummoxed when this man they had recalled as an oddball loner emerged as one of the most evilly charismatic personalities of all time. Plainly, charisma is an attribute that can be learned and acquired.

In charismatic leadership, the leader focuses attention on self. He/she seems to possess a certain charisma, to be inspired by supernatural powers. Often he/she is a mask for some other leader's style. The power appears to be drawn from intellectual strength and originality. Followers are converted to and are champions of the cause. Most charismatic leaders have a tendency toward authoritarian or bureaucratic styles.

This quality has been described by Max Weber as a magical aura with which people sometimes endow their leaders. It appears when a group has an emotional need for a person who, they feel, will make the right decision for them. The acts of charismatic leaders are typically unexamined. Their followers do not scrutinize their acts as they would those of their immediate supervisors. Charisma is not an objective assessment by the followers and normally requires a psychological distance between the followers and the leader. When charisma is assigned to a leader, the power and authority of the organization is enhanced.

5. Democratic or participative style

In the democratic style, all policies are derived from group decisions. The leader participates in the formation of policies but does not dominate group action. The group may decide with whom they will work and what tasks are to be accomplished by that policy. The democratic leadership style implies professional competence and personal sincerity. Individual growth is fostered through participation in all organizational operations.

Democratic or participative leader is primarily concerned with human relations and teamwork. Communication is open and usually goes both ways. He or she demonstrates spirit of collaboration and joint effort results in staff satisfaction. With this style of leadership, participation promotes acceptance of goals and goal commitment.

In all leadership styles, the key is decision making, the vehicle between planning processes and the systems' administration. J.W. Singleton (1972), writes that decisions can be made in many ways which are products of leadership style. He emphasizes the value of wide involvement and consultation. However, it is important that the leader realizes his/her personal accountability. The nature of the problem will dictate the extent of participation. The ultimate goal of leadership should be teamwork. This means cooperation and mutual discussion, thus typifying a democratic control at all levels of aspirations. The more people feel they are participating in what directly concerns them, the greater will be the spirit of cooperation throughout.

Similar to the research results for leadership behaviors, specific leadership styles appear to be more or less effective depending upon the situation (e.g., nature of tasks, organizational structure, subordinate characteristics). However, one result of research has been the recognition that, unlike traits or other specific characteristics, leadership behaviors and styles can be learned. The fact that a leader's personality or past experience helps form his or her preferred or "natural" style does not mean that leadership style is unchangeable or that a manager always uses the same style of leadership. Leadership styles range from very authoritarian to very permissive and frequently change according to the situation.

A manager may use one style (e.g., authoritarian) when responding to an emergency situation such as cardiac arrest. Another style (e.g., participation) may be used to encourage creative problem solving in developing a team strategy to care for a multi-problem patient or to generate ideas for use of a new procedure. The most effective leadership style for any leader is the one that best complements the organizational environment, the tasks to be accomplished, and the personal characteristics of the people involved in each situation. This is an *adaptive style* of leadership. (Sullivan et al., 1992).

Focusing on leadership styles does not explain which style will be most effective under which circumstances, nor do any of these approaches consider the specific and systematic effects of the leadership situation. This recurrent deficiency in leadership research eventually led to the development of several contingency theories of leadership that attempt to integrate leadership traits, leadership behaviors, and leadership situations in a unified theoretical framework. This framework helps us not only to understand more about effective leadership but also to predict what kinds of leader behaviors will be most effective in different circumstances.

Setting Your Own Style

As mentioned earlier, much has been written about leadership styles that explain how leaders think and act when managing workers. Leadership styles, attitudes and behaviors emanate from their general assumptions about their staff.

Chapter two explains two models of McGregor's Theory X and Theory Y. Theory X is when traditional leaders believe their workers are lazy, dislike work and responsibility, avoid work if not closely supervised or indifferent to organizational needs and goals will focus on monitoring and controlling staff in the organization in an effort to make them obey management's orders or face negative consequences. This attitude leads to task-oriented behaviors on the part of leaders, as opposed to relationship-oriented behaviors and such a leader will have a tendency to adopt a directive style. Directive leadership is characterized as take charge, one-directional, and single-handed decision-making by the leader. It also involves giving orders, establishing goals and methods of evaluation, setting time lines, defining roles, and establishing methods and processes for achieving the organization's goals (Northouse 2001).

Theory Y, according to McGregor is when the leaders have the opposite attitudes toward workers saying their workers want to take responsibility, they like challenging work, they desire opportunities for personal development and they want to help achieve organizational goals. Leaders who believe theory Y are likely to adopt relationship-oriented behaviors and will be inclined to use a participative or a delegative style of leadership. This relationship will result in supportive behaviors in which open communication, listening, praising, asking for input, and giving feedback are important (Northouse 2001). The main characteristic of participative style is involving other people in decision making and giving their ideas due consideration. In the delegative style, leaders derive considerable satisfaction from giving decision-making responsibilities to their staff (Brody 2000).

President Jon F. Kennedy's style suited him well. He came from a privileged background and definitely liked the finer things in life; thus, he wasn't about to make pretenses at being a plebian. You have to decide what style suits you best if you want to have a maximum impact as a leader.

Although your leadership style will reflect in how people perceived you, it is not just a personal thing. Kennedy didn't just work on his personal style, he worked to change how the presidency and the entire country was perceived. You need to also consider how your company, services, and products are perceived. Just as Kennedy's choices affected how the United States was perceived, so too do your choices as a leader reflect on how your company is perceived both internally and by the public. Barnes et al. (2005) gave the following tips on how to set your own style:

1. You will have a leadership style whether you like it or not; choose one that suits your personality and that best represents the company. Likewise, choose an image that works best for your company, services, and products. Sometimes changing the presentation of your products or your mission can change he way it is received. Consider, for example, Starbucks and its vision of a coffee shop. It's more like a café, with music, murals on the wall, and the coffee individually prepared for the customer. By changing the environment in which consumers use their products, Starbucks was able to change the way people perceive coffee as well as their relationship to the coffee provider.

2. Charisma is not a gift. Its basic elements can be learned. JFK's transformation from awkward young man to smooth, confident, "cool" young leader certainly shows this. If necessary, get professional help with both your personal image and that of your brand and product.

3. Pay attention to how others perceive you. Get an honest review of yourself - including your outward appearance and your style of presentation and communication. Then work on the individual elements, strengthening your weak points and making sure that they all add up to a style that supports your vision. Also, take the time to research how your products and company are perceived by your intended audience. If your brand or product needs a face-lift, take this seriously. If changes are needed, make them.

4. Don't lose sight of how style can help you set yourself apart as a leader. You don't need to have your own jet, but you can keep up with the latest fashions and trends. Don't be afraid to try new hairstyles or new clothing styles. They can help you stand out and get people to pay attention to what you have to say.

Fiedler's Contingency Theory

According to Sullivan et al. 1992, Fiedler articulated a contingency model of leadership effectiveness in the mid 1960s, which suggests that a manager's leadership style must be matched with the requirements of the situation to be effective (Fiedler, 1967). In Fiedler's theory, effectiveness is very carefully defined as the performance of the group itself, rather than a rating of the leader's effectiveness.

Fiedler differentiates two leadership styles, which he calls relationship-oriented and task-oriented leadership. These leadership styles are assessed with a questionnaire called the Least-Preferred Co-worker scale (LPC). The leader rates her least preferred co-worker on a set of 17 bipolar scales anchored at either end by adjectives (e.g., efficient-inefficient, friendly-rejecting). If the leader's least preferred co-worker is described in relatively positive terms, the leader is said to have an underlying relationship-oriented leadership style. If the least preferred co-worker is described in relatively unfavorable terms, then the individual is said to be basically a task-oriented leader.

Since Fiedler (1967) defines leadership as a process of influence, the leadership situation is described on a dimension that represents the relative ease or difficulty with which the leader can influence group members. This dimension, called situation favorability, has three components. The first is *leader-member* relations, the degree to which the leader enjoys the loyalty and support of subordinates. Second, *task structure* is the degree to which the task or finished product is clearly described and/or there are standard operating procedures that guarantee successful completion of the task and make it easy for the leader to determine how well the work has been performed. Finally, *position power* is the degree to which the leader is able to administer rewards and punishment by virtue of his or her position (i .e., legitimate power).

When leader-member relations are relatively good, when the task is highly structured, and when the leader has high position power, it is when the leader has high position power, it is relatively easy for the leader to influence the group toward the accomplishment of organizational objectives. Fiedler states that the leader-member relations component is the most important task; task structure, the next most important; and the leader's formal position power, the least important determinant of situation favorability.

Figure 4-1 illustrates the preferred leadership styles given different combinations of situational characteristics. According to Fiedler, a leader is most effective when the leadership style and the situation are marched, and he suggests that leaders should attempt to seek situations in which their predominant style is most appropriate. Should a mismatch occur, Fiedler suggests that the leader should attempt to change characteristics or the situation.

Combinations of situational characteristics

Leader member relations	Good	Good	Good	Good	Poor	Poor	Poor	Poor
Task structure	High	High	Low	Low	High	High	Low	Low
Position power	Strong	Weak	Strong	Weak	Strong	Weak	Strong	Weak
Preferred leadership styles	T	T	T	R	R	R	R	T

( ) T = Task-oriented style   ( ) R = Relationship-oriented style

John R. Schermerhorn, Jr., James G. Hunt, and Richard N. Osborn, Managing Organizational Behavior. (New York: John Wiley & Sons, 1982). Used by permission.

Figure 4-1 Predictions from Fiedler's Contigency Theory of Leadership

Path-Goal Theory and Leadership

Path-goal theory is an effort to apply a theory of human motivation and task performance to the realm of leadership effectiveness (House & Mitchell, 1974). A primary function of leadership is to motivate group members toward the attainment of organizational objectives. Path-goal theory suggests that this motivational functions carried out through leadership behaviors that remove obstacles to goal attainment and that make personal rewards for employees contingent upon attainment of those goals. Thus, a leader's function is to coach, guide, and provide performance incentives to ensure high work performance. Furthermore, the theory suggests that leader behavior directly affects group members' job satisfaction to the extent that the leader makes reward available and that the leader's behavior itself is a source of satisfaction to subordinates.

The motivational functions of leadership are built directly on the expectancy theory of work motivation. Briefly, employees are likely to work for rewards that they find attractive and that are likely to be awarded for successful performance. However, expectancy theory also suggests that expectancies (the perceived probability that effort will lead to high performance) must be strong before employees will be highly motivated. In this case, the manager's role is to clarify the nature of the task (the performance objective), to facilitate the staff member's attainment of that objective by providing the necessary resources and training, and to ensure the coordination and cooperation of other individuals required for successful task accomplishment.

Staff members interpret and respond to leader behavior in different ways depending upon such situational factors as subordinate characteristics, and characteristics of the task and environment. Specifically, subordinates' needs for achievement, affiliation, and autonomy; their ability to do the task (i.e., their job skills, knowledge, experience); and their personality traits (e.g., self-esteem) form a background or context within which leader behavior functions. Task and environmental characteristics also form a part of the background and include task structure (defined the same as in Fiedler's contingency model) and the degree of formalization imposed by the organization (e.g., written job descriptions, rules, standard operating procedures, performance standards). The effect of leadership behavior on subordinate satisfaction and effort depends upon the situation in which the leadership behavior occurs.

To accomplish these ends, path-goal theory specifies four leader behaviors.

(1) *Supportive leadership.*

Supportive leadership includes behaviors that consider the needs of subordinates, display concern for their well-being, and create a friendly climate in the work unit.

Behavior should be especially effective when subordinates perceive the job as boring, frustrating, stressful, or otherwise unpleasant. By trying to make the job more tolerable, the manager can directly affect employee satisfaction and perhaps even increase the desirability of the intrinsically motivating aspects of the work. Of course, when the work is perceived as interesting and enjoyable, supportive behavior does not necessarily increase either job satisfaction or motivation. When a staff has relatively high self-esteem or little fear failure, supportive leadership may have little or no effect on motivation.

(2) *Directive leadership.*

Directive leadership involves letting subordinates know what they are expected to do, giving specific guidance, asking them to follow rules and procedures, and scheduling and coordinating work efforts.

Provided staff do not already know what to do in a particular situation, directive leadership reduces role ambiguity (increasing expectancies) and increases the nurse's satisfaction. When the manager explains the relationship between performance and rewards, instrumentalities should increase. In addition, directive leadership can influence the desirability of outcomes for task success by changing the size or amount of rewards and punishment.

However, these effects will be successful only to the extent that the manager actually has control over specific rewards and punishment. Money is not the only (and often is not the best) incentive that can be used to successfully motivate staff members. Of course, the situation determines whether the directive manager is likely to increase staff motivation and satisfaction.

(3) *Achievement-oriented leadership.*

Achievement-oriented leadership includes setting challenging goals, seeking performance improvements, emphasizing excellent in performance, and showing confidence that subordinates will attain high levels of performance.

These leadership behaviors increase subordinates' confidence in their ability to achieve challenging goals. The higher the goal, the higher the performance, even when the goal is not always attained. Thus, the simple act of setting a goal, in addition to the expression of confidence in a staff member's ability, positively influences motivation. Of course, this is more effective whether task is fairly ambiguous and no repetitive, meaning it is relatively unstructured. Setting a specific goal not only clarifies what is to be done, but it also stimulates the development of strategies and plans for goal attainment, thus adding structure to an ambiguous task.

(4) *Participative leadership.*

In participative leadership, the manager consults with subordinates and takes their opinions and suggestions into account when making decisions.

Participative leadership behavior also has its greatest effect with instructed tasks. Participation gives staff members an opportunity to learn more about an unfamiliar task, and helping to develop both goals and strategies or plans to attain them directly affects employees understanding of what has to be done and how they must go about accomplishing it. Staff members who have high achievement or autonomy needs respond more favorably to participate leadership behavior than those who have lower needs for achievement and autonomy or who prefer structured tasks with little responsibility for decision making. In fact, the latter may find participation threatening and demanding, leading to less satisfaction with the manager. The effect of specific leadership behaviors on staff satisfaction and motivation depends directly upon the situation (particularly the degree of task structure) and employee characteristics.

Many health care procedures are highly reutilized and structured but many aspects of nursing such as patient relationships, orientating new staff members, and special projects are relatively unstructured. Thus, it is not always easy to prescribe a given leadership behavior that would be most effective for a particular task and employee combination. There is no substitute for good common sense and the judicious application of motivation and leadership principles. No formula exists that will work in every situation with every staff member or that can be applied across the board by anyone.

The task of leadership is complex and requires continuous problem solving. To use the path-goal theory of leadership effectively, the manager needs to engage constantly in diagnosing and predicting employee responses to given leadership acts. Path-goal theory provides a framework that casts some light on the effects of specific leadership behaviors and the types of situations in which such behaviors are or are not appropriate. It can be a very useful leadership tool for managers who regard their leadership responsibilities realistically.

Leadership by Walking Around

One effective style is leading by walking around (LBWA). When walking around and observing such things as staff interaction with customers, families, volunteers and employees, one can personally evaluate the quality of services being rendered. This is also an opportunity to see if the customers are having any problems and to physically inspect the building and equipment.

Leadership by wandering or walking around provides opportunity to the staff to speak with the administrator informally. It allows time to observe what is going on and to let the staff know the administrator is interested in them, the patients/customers, and the facility.

In making daily rounds the administrator can do naïve listening, gaining raw impressions of what is happening in the facility and sensing how things are going. Not enough time is available to get the paperwork done, meet all the other administrator requirements and still make time to walk daily around the facility, sensing its pulse? Sam Walton, the originator of Wal-Mart Corporation, visited every one of his stores at least once a year when he had 18 stores. By the early nineties he owned over 800 stores and he was till visiting each one at least once a year, rising cross country with Wal-Mart truck drivers having donuts at 3:00 a.m. He thought the check-out clerk to be the most important employee. Until his death in the early 1990s, every check-out clerk knew that sometime each year Mr. Sam might be the next customer waiting in the check-out line, observing how the customer ahead of him was being treated!

Wandering around the facility talking with patients/customers and staff appears to violate the traditional concept of chain command. The administrator is there to hear firsthand and to communicate firsthand. Ed Carson, a former airlines chairman, who led by walking around, took lots of notes on scraps of paper, but never told people down the line what to do or change. He never corrected on the spot what he disliked. But he did promise to get back to the person he had spoken with in a few days. He then discussed each situation with his department head and charted with her or him a course to resolve any problem. And after a few days he would check with the resident, visitor, or employee to see if appropriate action had been taken. He was practicing what he called "visible management" (Peters, 1987, p. 386).

According to Allen (1997), the basic benefits of leading by walking around are listening (finding out what's happening on the firing line), teaching (communicating the facility's values) and facilitating. Through LBWA the administrator can facilitate the work of employees by asking naïve questions, finding out what is frustrating the staff, then running interference and knocking down small hurdles for them. Only the facility that pays excessive attention to details can achieve excellence in patient/customer care. Quality of care is staff emulating their administrator, by paying attention to the details that lead to excellent care.

Leadership with Passion

According to the American Heritage Dictionary, 3rd Edition, passion is defined as "boundless enthusiasm". Jacques A. Nasser, President and CEO, Ford Motor Company, Dearborn, MI, said "I believe the people who are most successful are those who do what really interests them. There is no substitute for energy and enthusiasm."

Being a leader is an awesome responsibility. It takes talent to get the job. It takes drive to keep up with the job. But what it takes to be the job is passion.

According to Allen (1997), to be a successful administrator or leader of any organization over a sustained period of year requires that one be excited and passionate about the profession. Top performers in all fields have one quality in common: *passion*. Their drive and enthusiasm is what distinguishes excellent administrators. As numerous executive recruiters have observed, "The thing that makes the difference between a good manager and an inspiring, dynamic leader goes beyond competence. *It's passion*. That is the single quality that is going to lift a person head and shoulders above the rest" (Kriegel, 1991, p. 13).

Passion brings complete commitment to one's work: physical, emotional, and mental. It sustains the successful administrator through the outrages of regulation and an abusive public image of the field. Passion is contagious. An administrator enthusiastic about the work can inspire excitement in the nurses, physical therapists, occupational therapists, nursing assistants or other workers. Knowledge of the field, competence, and experience make a good manager, but a greater commitment gives one the necessary edge to provide the leadership necessary in today's health care industry for continuously improving the quality of the daily life of each patient. (Allen, 1997).

Passion is not a fleeting emotion. It resonates from one being to everyone in hearing and feeling range, and then is passed along for everyone to experience. Passion is contagious and that is why it is so important for a leader to possess it, and to express it with great energy and consistency.

CHAPTER FIVE

TEAM MANAGEMENT

"As for the differences of opinion upon speculative questions, if we wait till they are reconciled, the action of human affairs must be suspended forever. But neither are we to look for perfection in any one man, nor for agreement among many"

-- Junius

" I have no safe depository of the ultimate powers of society but the people themselves; and if we think them not enlightened enough to exercise their control with a wholesome discretion, the remedy is not to take it from them, but to inform their discretion by education."

-- Thomas Jefferson

"Innovation creates opportunity, quality creates demand, but teamwork makes it happen"

--Anonymous

The Manager as a Leader

Influencing team processes toward the attainment of organizational objectives is the direct responsibility of the manager. The manager can do a great deal to facilitate productivity in teams and promote the individual benefits of team membership. For example, through planning work and making assignments, the manager can increase the interdependence of team members. He or she can foster the sharing of common interests and exert considerable control over rewards and punishments for the attainment or non-attainment of work goals. The functions of team membership for individuals operate regardless of whether there is a formal leader, but the manager can do a great deal to foster effective individual and team performance by exercising constructive influence on these functions through leadership behavior. Indeed, this is one of the manager's primary roles in any organization.

The manager also acts as an observer of the direction in which the team is moving. He or she brings the attention of the staff members to the goal, clarifies issues in terms of how they relate to the unit's goals, and periodically evaluates the team's progress toward its goals. This evaluation and the subsequent planning and execution of team goals frequently includes the assistance of staff members.

Building Your Own Team

No one gets anything done alone. You must build a team. The presidential cabinet is designed to get representatives from various groups in one room to give critical advice and insights to the president. There are representatives from the departments of state, treasury, defense, health, labor, commerce, justice, and many other key groups that are fundamental to making the country run. Similarly, in business, executive advisory boards usually have representatives from various departments such as finance, HR, IT, marketing, and other key divisions. Although this is fairly common, getting a group of people together who will give constructive criticism and work together well, while still representing the needs of their division, is difficult - yet it is extremely important to achieve. This is especially critical when breaking into a new market, product, or service area, or when making any strategic decisions.

1. Make sure everything fits together. A leader not only creates an executive board, but encourages functional teams to do the same. This practice will help generate buy-in as well as keep all plans realistic. Consider, for example, IBM's approach to partnering. IBM not only has a team specializing in partnering with representatives from different parts of the company, it also insists that outside companies that want to partner with IBM be able to determine whether the potential partner will be a good fit or whether the plans will work.

2. Look for honesty and loyalty. Don't fall into the trap of seeking "yes men." Find people who bring new ideas to the table and who will

help you identify potential problems from the outset. President J.F. Kennedy chose men for his team who were not afraid to speak their minds. At the same time, they were also loyal. This crucial combination will ensure that you get the best ideas possible, and a dedicated team to back them up.

3. Overlook personal quirks. Don't let someone's personal quirks blind you to his or her virtues. It's tempting to leave certain personalities off advisory boards because they "hold things up" or because of personal disputes. Understand that a certain amount of dissention is necessary to create superior strategies. John Barnes, (2005) asserted, you need people to think outside of the box and to challenge assumptions that come out of homogeneous groups. If the people on your team are doing what you need done, overlook the rest. If the individual's quirks are particularly disruptive, you may need to reconsider. But if you end up removing that person, try to find a suitable replacement.

4. Choose qualified people. Don't be afraid to bring in people who are personally close to you, but make sure they have the ability to do the job. President Kennedy was able to bring in his brother Robert Kennedy because he was more than loyal and trusted; he was qualified. If your people are qualified, no one will complain about unfair practices.

5. Praise in public and criticize in private.

6. Be more curious and less critical. Ask why and how as opposed to ranting about what should have been done. An eager ear provides greater benefits than a tart tongue.

7. Pull and don't push. To lead you must get out in front. And you must lead by pulling, not pushing.

8. Check your integrity. A recent study reported that only 47 percent of American employees saw the leaders of their companies as people of high personal integrity. And that was before the Enron, Arthur

Andersen, Global Crossing, HealthSouth, and WorldCom scandals, among others came to light. How can you build a passionate team to strive toward your vision when the members of the team don't trust you?

9. Foster positive emotions. One of the leader's vital jobs is to make people feel good. This is especially true during the bad times, the hard times, the down times. Do your best to help individuals deal with negative emotions and to stimulate positive emotions.

10. Strive to understand others. Realize that people don't leave their feelings at home when they come to work, and that it is almost impossible not to bring the stress of work into the home.

11. Show confidence in people. A good way to motivate individuals is to ask them for their opinion and input. This demonstrates your faith in their ability and competence, and stimulates them to work to be worthy of your concern.

12. Celebrate diversity. It is imperative to never forget that your team is a collection of individuals with different backgrounds, cultures, styles, ambitions, and needs.

13. Unleash potential. Team success hinges on your success in tapping into the potential of each and every member of the team.

14. Set the tone by creating an environment of infectious enthusiasm where the expectation of excellence permeates every facet of the business. Have passion, compassion, intensity and encourage or reward individuals to help maximize their creativity and talent and provide them with a great sense of self-worth.

15. You need to care about the people with whom you work each day. Caring involves compromising to ensure participation. Apologizing when you are wrong. Recognize to learn from your failures and celebrate your success. Empathize by genuinely concerned with your staff's feelings and circumstances.

What is a Team

A team is a collection of individuals who share a common set of norms, who generally have differentiated roles among themselves, and who interact with one another to jointly pursue common objectives (Steers, 1984). *Command teams* are organized to achieve organizational goals. The supervisor of the team has line authority over the team members.

A *task team* is several persons who work together with or without an assigned leader to perform certain tasks. A task team can also be a command team but usually there are several task teams in a department or there are task teams that include members from several departments, such as a patient care team that includes a nurse, a physician, a dietitian, and a social worker.

There are also special teams such as *committees or task forces* that are formed to deal with specific issues involving several departments. These could include a committee that is responsible for safety or a task force assigned to develop better procedures. There are many committees used in health care institutions on which nurse managers serve, including nursing education committees, nursing policy and procedures committees, disaster committees, and patient care evaluation committees.

Formal teams can be lateral, vertical, or diagonal: members from the same work team, from different levels in the organization, or from different departments in the organization. Task teams can be vertical, horizontal, or diagonal while command team are vertical groups. Likert (1961) suggests that an important role of a command team leader such as a nurse manager is to serve a link with teams higher in the organization. This link facilitates problem solving and communication in the organization. Teams can be permanent or temporary. Command teams, teams, and committees usually are permanent teams while task forces are often temporary. Each different type of team presents opportunities and difficulties for the manager.

Leadership roles in a team are very important and can be either formal or informal. For example, the manager leads the staff team (formal) but may also serve as a leader in an informal grouping of managers. The leader's influence on team processes and the ability of the team to work together often determines whether the team is effective in accomplishing organizational and personal goals, regardless of the formality of the leader's role. This chapter presents how managers can effectively manage teams by presenting a model of team processes and then discussing team decision making, teams and team building, and the management of committees and task forces.

Team Management

The development of teams is an inevitable part of human activity and, therefore, teams are a fact of life in all organizations. Because staff nurses work in close proximity and frequently depend upon each other to accomplish their jobs, the character or climate of team interaction is extremely important. A viable atmosphere in which staff members feel free to talk about what concerns them, to critique and offer suggestions, and to experiment with new behaviors without threat can only be maintained in a work group that is warm, supportive, and relatively unhindered by interpersonal conflicts and political infighting. Maintaining such an atmosphere or climate is an important task for any manager. Besides meeting with their staff, managers are often in other team settings with their super ordinates and other managers, or in committees and task forces. Understanding the nature of teams and team processes, how teams develop, how they influence organizational performance, how they influence member satisfaction, and how leaders can influence their performance are essential to the effectiveness of a manager.

According to Sullivan et al., 1992, there are two primary types of teams. *Informal teams* evolve naturally as a result of people's interaction within an organization. They are informal in the sense that they are not part of any organizational design. An example is a team of people who regularly eat lunch together. *Formal teams* are work units developed by the organization either temporarily or permanently to accomplish organizational tasks. This chapter focuses on formal teams, such as a departmental (or command) teams, task teams, task forces, committees, and informal organizational teams which will be discussed later.

Team Development

Teams are groups established to perform organizational tasks requiring the diverse skills and the interaction and cooperation of the team members to achieve these tasks. Teams have command or line authority to perform tasks and membership is based on the specific skills the individual can offer to accomplish the team's task. Teams can be lateral, vertical, or diagonal in member composition. They can have a short life or can exist over long periods of time. Not all work groups are teams. For example, co-acting groups, where members perform their tasks independently of each other, are not teams, nor are competing groups, where members compete with each other for resources to perform their tasks or where members compete for recognition. Specific difficulties teams experience include goal confusion, hidden agendas, territoriality, disagreement over procedures, competition among team members, inter-group conflict, and a no supportive climate.

Team building is a popular organizational development (OD) technique that can be used to overcome some of these difficulties. OD team building activities include using outside intervention to build team cohesiveness. For example, McGraw-Hill (CRM/McGraw-Hill, 1983) has a Task-Oriented Team Development Program designed to be self-administered by the team leader and members themselves. They have also developed an excellent film, *Team Building* which can be used by a facilitator to help improve team performance. The various volumes of a Handbook of Structured Experiences for Human Relations Training (J.W. Pfeiffer and J.E. Jones, Iowa City, IA: University Associates) also provide many useful team-building exercises. Intervention strategies are covered in depth in Team Building: Blueprints for Productivity and Satisfaction (Reddy and Jemison,1988).

A leadership team is more effective than just one leader. Leaders who build teams have vision and are willing to hire people better than themselves. They are wise leaders because they share their staff into a team. They are secured when they empower their teams. They show experience when they listen to their teams and they are productive leaders when they understand that one is too small a number to achieve greatness (Maxwell, 2005).

To develop effective teams, four conditions are necessary: The group must have mutually agreed objectives; the group members must depend on each other's experiences, abilities, and commitment; group members must be committed to team effort; and the group must be accountable as a unit within the organization (Patten, 1979). Team-building techniques can be used to create these conditions. Team-building activities can also be used to overcome one of the most important difficulties in managing teams (and task forces) in organizations, which is that teams must go through the normal stages of group development (form, storm, norm, perform, and adjourn or reform) quickly and are expected to perform as a high level immediately. Team-building techniques also can be used to intervene in traditional work groups that are experiencing problems or in any other type of group such as quality circles, task forces, and committees.

The first and most important activity in team building is diagnosis. Questions must be asked about the group's climate, including its mission and goals; the group's organization, including group members' roles, group procedures, and decision-making style; the group's interpersonal relationships in the group, including members' feelings about each other; and the group's relations with other groups.

Team Development typically follows a set pattern of activities: they *form*, or come together; they *storm* or develop leaders and roles; they *norm*, or define goals and rules for acceptable behavior; they *perform*, or agree on basic purposes and activities and start working; and they *adjourn or reform* (Tuckman & Jensen, 1977). These phases of team development are true for both formal and informal teams.

In the initial stage of forming, team members are cautious in approaching others, become familiar with each other, and begin an understanding of the requirements of team membership. At this stage the members are often quite dependent on the team leader. As the team begins to develop, the second stage, storming occurs, where conflict arises among the members of the team on issues that are important to the members. During this stage, members who often look for power begin to define what are or are not acceptable behaviors and attitudes and become organized into an effective unit. In the perform stage, the energy of the team members is channeled into the work. Good communication occurs among the members, and they have a relaxed atmosphere of sharing.

The fifth stage is either adjourning (the team has achieved its purpose) or reforming when some major change takes place in the membership or environment of the team, causing the team to recycle through the previous four stages.

Questions frequently asked include:

1. Do the members understand and accept the goals of the group? Is there any goal confusion? Goal confusion occurs when the team is unsure of its goals or there is disagreement over these goals.

2. Do the members have any hidden agendas that interfere with the group's goal attainment? Hidden agendas are members' individual goals that are not shared with the group as a whole and keep the members from being committed and enthusiastic team members.

3. Is the leadership role being handled adequately?

4. Does each member understand and accept his or her role in the group?

5. How does the group make decision?

6. How does the group handle conflict? Are conflicts dealt with through avoidance, forcing, accommodating, compromising, competing, or collaborating methods?

7. What feelings do members have about each other?

8. Do members trust and respect each other?

9. What is the relationship between the team and other units in the organization?

Only after diagnosing the problems of the team can the team leader take actions to improve team functioning. Survey feedback forms can be used to improve teams. The results of the survey are discussed by the group and action steps are defined to overcome these problems. After a period of time another survey is taken to see if change has occurred and whether the process needs to be repeated. An outside intervention specialist can be brought in to conduct team-building sessions including holding a confrontation meeting to address team problems.

Argyris (1965) summarizes the characteristics of an effective team:

1. Contributions made within the group are additive.

2. The group moves forward as a unit; there is a sense of team spirit, high involvement.

3. Decisions are made by consensus.

4. Commitment to decisions by most members is strong.

5. The group continually evaluates itself.

6. The group is clear about its goals

7. Conflict is brought out into the open and handled.

8. Alternative ways of thinking about solutions are generated.

9. Leadership tends to go to the individual best qualified, and

10. Feelings are dealt with openly.

General Guidelines for Conducting Meetings

To conduct a successful meeting, the leader should spend time thinking about the purpose of the meeting; preparing an agenda; determining who should attend; making assignments prior to group meetings, including determining who should take minutes; and selecting an appropriate time and place for the meeting. An agenda should be established for meetings ahead of time and sent to the participants. The ideal committee size is five to seven persons. Having too few or too many members can limit the effectiveness of a committee or task force. It is helpful to limit membership to persons with similar status, as large status differences among committee members can impede communication.

Meetings should be held in spaces where interruptions can be controlled and at a time when there is some natural time limit to the meeting, such as late in the morning or afternoon when lunch or dinner make natural time barriers. In addition, meetings should start and finish on time. Starting late positively reinforces latecomers while punishing those who arrive on time or early. Locking the door at the appointed time or "fining" latecomers can discourage such behavior. If it is the leader who is late, informing him or her as to the cost of starting meetings late can be effective.

The behavior of each member may be positive, negative, or neutral in relationship to the group's goals. Members may contribute very little or they may use the group to fill personal needs. Some members may assume most of the responsibility for the group action, thereby "helping" the less participative members to be noncontributory.

According to David C. Gustafson, appropriate or key behaviors for group meetings that can facilitate the group's action include:

* Coming prepared with necessary information

* Listening to others with an open mind

* Contributing information, ideas, and opinions.

* Asking other members for ideas and opinions

* Requesting clarification of information.

* Recognizing opposing points of view.

* Keeping remarks on the topic.

* Be willing to state disagreement and give rationale.

* Volunteering to help with the implementation of decisions when appropriate.

Leadership at Meetings

A leader can play an effective role in conducting meetings by ensuring that the 12 leadership roles shown in figure 5-1 are present. Even though a leader's personality and value systems might make it difficult for him or her to perform all of those roles, the leader is still responsible to make sure that these various task and group relations functions do occur, even if they are performed by other members.

A leader can also increase effectiveness by not letting one person dominate discussion, separating idea generation from evaluation; encouraging members to refine and develop the ideas of others (a key to the success of brainstorming); recording problems, ideas, and solutions on a blackboard or flip chart; frequently summarizing information and the group's progress to date and encouraging further discussion; and bringing disagreements out into the open where they may be reconciled. The leader is also responsible for drawing out the members' hidden agendas (personal needs individuals bring to a group that are not disclosed to the group but influence the members' contributions) so these do not interfere with group decision making.

Task Functions Of a Group Leader

1. **Initiating:** Proposing tasks or goals; defining a group problem; suggesting a procedure or ideas for solving a problem.
2. **Information or opinion seeking:** Requesting facts; seeking relevant information about group concern; asking for suggestions or ideas.
3. **Information giving:** Starting a belief; providing relevant information about group concern; opinion giving suggestions or ideas.
4. **Clarifying:** Elaborating, interpreting, or reflecting ideas and suggestions; clearing up confusions; indicating alternatives and issues before the group; giving examples.
5. **Summarizing:** Pulling together related ideas; restating suggestions after group has discussed them; offering a decision or conclusion for the group; giving examples.
6. **Consensus testing:** Sending up "trial balloons" to see if group is nearing a conclusion; checking with group to see how much greement has been reached.

Group relations functions

7. **Encouraging:** Being friendly, warm, and responsive to others; accepting others and their contributions; regarding others by giving them an opportunity for recognition.
8. **Expressing group feelings:** Sensing feelings, moods, relationships within the group; sharing one's own feelings with other members.
9. **Harmonizing:** Attempting to reconcile disagreements; reducing tension; getting people to explore their differences.
10. **Modifying:** When the leader's own idea or status is involved in a   conflict, offering to modify this position; admitting error; disciplining themselves to maintain group cohesion.
11. **Gate-keeping:** Attempting to keep communication channels open; facilitating the participation of others; suggesting procedures for sharing opportunity to discuss group problems.
12. **Evaluating:** Evaluating group functioning and production; expressing standards for group to achieve; measuring results; evaluating degree of group commitment.

Sullivan, Eleanor J., Effective Management Nursing, 3rd Edition, © 1992, p 268. Reprinted by Permission of Pearson Education, Inc., Upper Saddle River, NJ.

Figure 5-1: The Functions of a Group Leader

Team Cohesiveness and Productivity

Productivity in a nursing unit includes the extent to which work is completed at the end of each shift and patient care and satisfaction are good. Productivity is influenced by groups, especially cohesive teams. *Cohesiveness* is the degree to which the members are attracted to the team. It includes how much the team members enjoy participating in the team and how much they are willing to contribute to the team. In highly cohesive teams where powerful norms are established on how hard members should work, uniformity exists among team members' productivity. When cohesiveness is low, wide differences can exist in employees' productivity. Teams can restrict productivity, especially when they oppose the organization's leaders.

Cohesiveness is also related to homogeneity of interests, values, attitudes, and background factors. Several propositions on group interaction and cohesiveness are shown in the following list.

1. The greater the opportunity or requirements for interactions, the greater the likelihood of interaction occurring (Homans, 1961).

2. The more frequent the interaction among people, the greater the likelihood of their developing positive feelings for one another (Homans, 1961).

3. The greater the positive feelings among people, the more frequently they interact (Homans, 1961).

4. The more frequent the interactions required by the job, the more likely that social relationships and behavior will develop along with task relationships and behavior (Homans, 1961).

5. The more attractive the team, the more cohesive it is (Festinger, Schcter & Black, 1950).

6. The more cohesive the team, the more influence it has on its members. The less certain and clear a team's norms and standards

are, the less control it has over its members (Festinger, Schacter & Black, 1950; Homans, 1961).

7. The greater the similarity in member attitudes and values brought to the team, the greater the likelihood of cohesion (Homans, 1961).

8. Team cohesion is increased by the existence of a super-ordinate goal (an overarching goal to which team members subscribe) accepted by the members (Sherif, 1967).

9. Team cohesion is increased by the perceived existence of a common enemy (Blake & Mouton, 1961).

10. Team cohesion increases in proportion to the status of the team relative to other teams in the system (Cartwright & Zander, 1968).

11. Team cohesion increases in proportion to the status of the team relative to other teams in the system (Cartwright & Zander, 1968).

12. Team cohesion increases when there is low frequency of required external interactions (Homans, 1961).

13. The more easily and frequently member differences are settled in a way satisfactory to all members, the greater is team cohesion (Deutsch, 1968).

14. Team cohesion increases under conditions of abundant resources (Blake & Mouton, 1961).

15. The more cohesive the team, the more similar is the output of individual members (Homans, 1961).

16. The more cohesive the team, the more it tries to enforce compliance with its norms about productivity (Blake & Mouton, 1961).

17. The greater the cohesion of the team, the higher productivity is if the team supports the organization's goals, and the lower productivity is if the team resists the organization's goals. (Zaleznik, Christensen & Roethlisberger, 1958).

18. A cohesive team by definition has a high overall level of satisfaction (Blake & Mouton, 1961).

Cohesive teams are more likely to develop where there are shared values and beliefs, where individuals have similar goals and tasks, where individuals have to interact together to achieve these tasks, where team members work in the same unit and on the same shift, and where team members have specific needs that can be satisfied by the team. Team cohesiveness is also influenced by the formal reward system. Teams whose members are treated equally, have similar pay, and have similar tasks, especially where the tasks require interaction among the members, are cohesive. Similarities in educational experiences, social class, sex, age, and ethnicity that lead to similar attitudes strengthen team cohesiveness.

Cohesiveness can lead to social pressure and conformity. Highly cohesive teams can demand and enforce conformity to their norms regardless of their practical or effectiveness. This makes it more difficult for the manager to influence staff when the team norms deviate from his or her expectations or goals. In addition, teams can affect absenteeism and turnover. Teams with high levels of cohesiveness exhibit lower turnover and absenteeism than teams with low levels of cohesiveness.

Reasons Individuals join Teams.

1. *Security* -- People want protection from threats; teams provide social support.

2. *Proximity* -- People often come together because they are located together.

3. *Group goals* -- People form teams to pursue goals that cannot be accomplished alone.

4. *Economics* -- People often form teams (e.g., collective bargaining organizations) to pursue economic self-interest.

5. *Social needs* -- People often join teams because they want to belong or be needed or because they want to lead.

6. *Self-esteem needs* -- People often join prestigious teams to increase their self-esteem.

7. *Development and Growth* -- People often join teams that provide learning opportunities by increasing individual skills or abilities, by the range of resources available, or by the ability to function effectively as a team in changed circumstances. (Cohen et al., 1988).

Disadvantages of Team Decision Making

Team decision making also has disadvantages in that it takes time and resources and can lead to conflict among members. Team decision making also can lead to the emergence of benign tyranny within the group. Those members who are less informed or confident may allow stronger members to present all solutions and decisions. This sets the stage for a power struggle between the manager and a few assertive team members. Social loafing and free riding can also occur in teams (Harkins, Latane & Williams, 1980). *Social loafing* refers to individuals' tendency to produce below their maximum capabilities in a team. *Free riding* occurs when a loafer receives the full benefits of team membership. Social loafing is more likely to occur as the team becomes larger. Team decision making can also be affected by groupthink.

Teamthink is a negative phenomenon that occurs in cohesive teams. The team members think alike, have similar prejudices and blind spots such as shared stereotypes of outsiders, tend to want to achieve consensus and harmony, and fail to engage in critical thinking. Teamthink occurs when there are shared norms or expectations that (a) the team is invulnerable to outside pressure; (b) the team believes itself to be morally right, which inclines members to ignore the ethical and moral consequences of their decisions; (c) the team rationalizes warnings and other forms of negative feedback; (d) there is direct pressure upon any individual who expresses doubts about the team's shared illusions or who questions the validity of arguments supporting an alternative favored by the majority; (e) there is self-censorship, in which individuals are pressured to conform to the team consensus; and (f) a shared illusion of unanimity exists within the team (Janis, 1982). These norms and expectations interfere with critical thinking and can make team decision making ineffective.

Janis suggests several approaches to prevent teamthink in cohesive teams, which are shown in the following list.

1. The leader of a policy-forming team should assign the role of critical evaluator to each member, encouraging the team to give high priority to airing objections and doubts.
   This practice needs to be reinforced by the leader's acceptance of criticism of his or her own judgments to discourage the members from soft-pedaling their disagreements.

2. The leaders in an organization's hierarchy, when assigning a policy-planning mission to a team, should be impartial instead of stating preferences and expectations at the outset.

3. The organization should routinely follow the administrative practice of setting up several independent policy-planning and evaluation teams to work on the same policy question, each carrying out its deliberations under a different leader.

4. The team should from time to time divide into two or more subteams to meet separately, under different chairpersons, and then come together to hammer out their differences.

5. Each member of the policy-making team should discuss periodically the team's deliberations with trusted associates in his or her own unit of the organization and report back their reactions.

6. One or more outside experts or qualified colleagues within the organization who are not core members of the policy-making team should be invited to each meeting on a staggered basis and should be encouraged to challenge the views of the core members.

7. At every meeting devoted to evaluating policy alternatives, at least one member should be assigned the role of devil's advocate.

8. Whenever the policy issue involves relations with a rival, time should be spent surveying all warning signals from the rivals and constructing alternative scenarios of the rivals' intentions.

9. After reaching a preliminary consensus about what seems to be the best policy alternative, the policy-making teamp should hold a "second chance" meeting at which every member is expected to express as vividly as possible all residual doubts and to rethink the entire issue before making a definite choice (Janis, 1982: pp.262-271).

Yet, it is important for managers to understand that conflict is not always dysfunctional and dissent must be allowed if good decisions are to be made.

A technique resulting in less teamthink is the use of *dialectical inquiry*. Dialectical inquiry uses a formal debate between advocates of a plan and others who propose a counter plan. This technique formalizes conflict by allowing disagreement, encourages the exploration of alternative solutions, and reduces the emotional aspects of conflict (Cosier & Schwenk, 1990). This approach can be used regardless of a manager's feelings. The benefits from this method come from the presentation and debate of the basic assumptions underlying proposed courses of action. Any false or misleading assumptions become apparent, and the process promotes better understanding of problems and leads to higher levels of confidence in decisions. But the method does have some potential drawbacks. It can lead to an emphasis on who won the debate rather than what the best decision is, or it can lead to inappropriate compromise (Cosier & Schwenk, 1990).

When to Use Teams for Decision Making

Vroom and Jago have developed a model for deciding whether to use a team for decision making (Vroom & Jago, 1988). In practice, the degree of participation is determined by several factors: (a) who initiates ideas; (b) the extent that subordinate support is required for implementation of a solution; (c) how completely an employee carries out each phase of decision making-diagnosing, finding alternatives, estimating consequences, and making choices;

(d) how much weight the manager attaches to the ideas received; and (e) the amount of knowledge the manager has about the matter. Likert (1961) has found that when individuals are allowed to participate they function more productively, and implementing solutions becomes easier because of the shared problem solving.

Generally teams should be used for decision making when time is available for a team decision but there is a deadline, the problem is complex or unstructured, the team members share the organization's goals, there is need for acceptance of the decision or at least understanding of the decision to implement it properly, and the process will not lead to unacceptable conflict among team members.

Types of Decision-Making Teams

The different types of decision-making teamss include ordinary interacting teams, nominal group technique, brainstorming team, statistical aggregation, the Delphi technique, and quality circles (Levine & Moreland, 1990; Murninghan, 1981; and Ouchi, 1981). Each type of team has advantages and disadvantages in decision making.

Ordinary interacting teams usually have a designated formal leader, but they can be leaderless. Most task groups and committees are this type.

They usually begin with a statement of the problem by the team leader followed by an open, instructed discussion of the problem. Normally the final decision is made by consensus, but the decision can also be by vote of the majority, by vote of a significant minority, by an expert, by the leader, or by some authority figure after the team makes a recommendation. Interacting teams enhance the cohesiveness and esprit de corps among team members. Participants are able to build strong social ties and there will be commitment to the solution decided upon by the team.

Ordinary teams are often dominated by one or a few members. If the team is highly cohesive, its decision-making ability can be affected by teamthink. Excessive time may be spent dealing with social-emotional relationships, reducing the time spent on the problem and making it difficult to come to a consensus. Ordinary teams may reach compromise decisions that may not really satisfy any of the participants. Because of these problems, ordinary teams are very dependent on the skills of the team leader.

Two techniques have been developed to allow input from various individuals while avoiding some of the disadvantages of ordinary teams: the nominal team technique (NTT) and the Delphi technique. The *nominal team technique*, developed by Van de Ven and Delbecq (1974) is a structured team decision-making process and is a team in name only because no social exchange is allowed between members. NTT consists of (a) silently generating ideas in writing, (b) round-robin feedback from group members to record each idea in a terse phrase on a flip chart, (c) discussing each recorded idea for clarification and evaluation, and (d) voting individually on priority ideas, with the team decision being mathematically derived through rank ordering or rating using the team's decision rule.

The second method, which isn't very common in health care administration, is the *Delphi technique*. Judgments on a particular topic are systematically gathered from participants who are physically separated and do not meet face to face. These are collected through a set of carefully designed sequential questionnaires interspersed with a summary of information and opinions derived from previous questionnaires. The process can include many iterations but normally does not exceed three. This technique can rely on the input of experts widely dispersed geographically. It can be used to evaluate the quality of research proposals or to make predictions about the future based on current scientific knowledge. This technique is useful when expert opinions are needed and the experts are geographically separated, but it is costly and time-consuming.

On fact-finding problems with no known solution, the NGT and the Delphi technique are superior to the ordinary team technique, and satisfaction of team members is highest in NGT (Van de Ven & Delbecq, 1974). Both NGT and the Delphi technique minimize the chances of more vocal and persuasive members influencing the less forceful persons and allow the opportunity to think through ideas independently.

Two other team techniques are statistical aggregation and brainstorming. Like the Delphi technique statistical aggregation does not require a team meeting. Individuals are polled regarding a specific problem and their responses are tallied. It is a very efficient technique but it is limited to a narrow range of problems: those for which a quantifiable answer can be readily obtained. One disadvantage of both statistical aggregation and the Delphi technique is that no opportunity exists for team members to strengthen their interpersonal ties.

In brainstorming, team members meet together and are encouraged to generate as many diverse ideas as possible without consideration of their practicality or feasibility. A premium is placed on generating lots of ideas as quickly as possible and on coming up with unusual ideas. In addition, and most important, members are asked not to critique the ideas as they are proposed. Evaluation takes place after all the ideas have been generated. Members are encouraged to "piggyback" on each other's ideas. These sessions are very enjoyable, but are often less successful because the members violate the three rules and, as a result, the meetings shift from the ordinary interacting team format. NTT can be used to overcome some of the problems of the brainstorming technique but it is not as exciting to the participants.

Quality circles are another type of group used in participatory decision making. Quality circles, adapted from Ouchi's Theory Z (Ouchi, 1981), have been successful in this country as well as in Japan. This style, which can easily be adapted to administration, is based on trust and worker's involvement in decisions that affect them. The system emphasizes consensus-based decision making and a strong commitment to the goals of the organization. The desired results are increased job commitment, higher productivity, and lower turnover.

Quality circles have been used in health care situations, but their use requires total organizational decision and commitment. Managers would not ordinarily use this technique unless their organization was using it. However, it may be useful to understand the process.

As an example, staff on each department are divided into circles of eight or ten individuals with a facilitator appointed for each circle. The facilitators form another circle, which interfaces with circles at higher and lower levels, so reciprocal representation exists at all levels. Circles are thoroughly disciplined operations committed to training, team skills, and rigorous step-by-step improvement procedures. There is continuous discussion within the circles whenever a policy or procedural change is made, until a true consensus has been achieved.

Many management decisions are made in circles, and no decision is final until every member has had a part in the decision and agrees with the outcome. This can be a time-consuming process, but once consensus is reached, implementation is instantaneous and the net effect is increased productivity. In other forms of participatory decision making, a majority wins, leaving a dissatisfied, obstinate minority who may sabotage implementation. In consensus-based decision making, everyone feels a part of the process, has a voice in the decision, and is therefore a winner. While research on quality circles in health care is limited, one study has shown improved morale, decreased alienation, and greater incentives for unified productivity when quality circles were introduced (Moore et al., 1982).

Likert's System theory also closely approximates management by consensus. The research he and his colleagues have done supports the conclusion that the more the employees are allowed to participate, the greater the likelihood of superior performance (Likert, 1961). However, the most important limitation to its use is the extent to which it is germane to the Japanese culture (Smith, Reinow & Reid,1984). The work ethic in Japan puts high value on team-work, while in the United States, independent accomplishment is more highly valued. Thus, team decision making is very workable in Japanese settings and less so in U.S. ones. Another important element is that quality circles may be more useful when members represent various interacting units or disciplines, especially in health care. This model, because of the greater participation it provides and the long-term rewards built into the system, certainly needs to be evaluated in terms of health care management. It shows potential for use in an area where innovative management is badly needed.

The manager needs to assess the team members in the organization to determine if a participatory process would enhance decision making. If staff show similar qualifications and work well together, perhaps quality circles could be instituted with success. If the team is extremely diversified and individualistic, however, NTT might be beneficial, or, if creativity is required, brainstorming might be beneficial. If the requisite leadership skills are available, then the ordinary team technique could be used. It is essential to match the decision-making method with the capabilities of the staff.

CHAPTER SIX

EFFECTIVE DELEGATION

"Don't be afraid to take big steps. You can't cross a chasm in two small jumps"

-- David Lloyd George

"There are four steps to accomplishment:
- *Plan Purposefully*
- *Prepare Prayerfully*
- *Proceed Positively*
- *Pursue Persistently"*

--Author Unknown

Leadership is an interactive task requiring continuous problem solving and a great deal of teamwork. Unfortunately, research shows that many managers have considerable difficulty building an effective team. In fact, most managers treat a few subordinates as members of a trusted cadre, or "in group," while others are relegated to the "out group" comprising the rest of the staff. In-group employees enjoy more frequent communication with the manager, are more likely to be "in-the-know" about organizational plans and activities, and are far more likely to be consulted when decisions regarding the department or unit are made. Not surprisingly, these individuals have higher job satisfaction and are generally given higher performance ratings than out-group employees (Dansereau, Graen, & Haga, 1975). It should not be surprising that close teamwork is very difficult to develop when managers "play favorites" with some staff members.

Because staff nurses work in close proximity and frequently depend upon each other to accomplish their jobs, the character or climate of leadership and group interaction is extremely important. An effective group atmosphere is one in which staff members feel free to talk about what concerns them, to critique and offer suggestions, and to experiment with new behaviors without threat. Such an atmosphere can only be maintained in a work group that is warm and supportive and is relatively unhindered by interpersonal conflicts, favoritism, and political in-fighting. Maintaining such an atmosphere or climate is a difficult leadership task.

One of the best ways to develop a supportive climate is to foster a feeling of group cohesiveness. Cohesiveness is the degree of attraction that each group member feels toward the group. Strong group cohesiveness leads to a feeling of "we" as being more important than self-centered "I" feelings and ensures a higher degree of cooperation and interpersonal support among group members. The "catch-22" in group cohesiveness is whether the group norms, the informal or often unstated rules and expectations regarding appropriate behavior for group members, support or subvert organizational objectives. High group cohesiveness fosters either higher or lower individual performance, depending upon group norms.

Groups lacking cohesiveness have difficulty getting much accomplished because members' efforts are more likely to go in scattered directions than to be focused toward the attainment of goals and outcomes valued by the group. Fortunately for the nurse manager, the nursing profession supports high standards of patient care, and nursing education induces values and patterns of behavior that encourage those high standards. However, this is true only to a degree; some work units are more successful than others in providing patient care because of differences in group cohesiveness.

The manager can foster high group cohesiveness primarily through managing group interaction patterns. Cohesiveness is a process of interpersonal attraction, and this attraction is influenced by a number of characteristics (Mitchell & Larson, 1987). For example, the physical proximity of some group members makes it likely that they will develop a friendship. Furthermore, the frequency of interaction and the expectation of future interaction increase the likelihood that individuals will be attracted to those who are physically nearby.

Of particular importance is managing communication processes to facilitate unit effectiveness. The manager who maintains a high degree of information power, for instance, controls not only what information is received but who receives it, funneling it down to specific, individual staff. This represents a highly centralized communication structure in contrast to one in which the nurse manager encourages a high degree of participative group problem solving. In participative groups, each individual has the opportunity, and is encouraged, to communicate frequently with anyone and everyone in the group.

The relative effectiveness of centralized versus decentralized communication networks depends upon the structure of the task (defined in Fiedler's contingency model and in path-goal theory). For every complex and unstructured problems, a decentralized communication structure produces solutions in less time and with fewer errors and enhances member satisfaction more than a highly centralized structure. For rather simple problems or tasks that are more structured, a centralized communication network may yield faster results and have fewer errors than a decentralized structure.

In addition, members of groups who have a history of success with a task are attracted to each other more than if they have not been successful;: success breeds attraction. When group members have a common goal, there is higher attraction than when they have different goals. A common goal provides a bond around which interaction and friendships develop. In addition, the ability to influence group decision processes increases attraction to the group. Managers can influence all of these factors through task design, work assignments, and the decision-making/leadership processes they implement in the department.

The greatest contributions to interpersonal attraction come from the personal characteristics of group members. People are attracted to those whom they perceive to be similar to themselves. Similarities in race, education, background, attitudes, and values all increase the interpersonal attractiveness of group members. People seem to like each other because they are common goals, because other people can be rewarding in a variety of ways, or because they are similar on a number of important dimensions. This increased attraction influences group processes and results.

In general, the greater the attraction, the greater the influence. In job satisfaction research, results are quite clear: Increased attraction (cohesiveness) leads to increased satisfaction, However, performance is increased only if the norms and goals of the group support the organization's objectives. Cohesive groups can make or break the manager's leadership efforts and should always be taken into account as part of the leadership situation. In particular, communication networks (who talks to whom) have considerable implication for both performance and job satisfaction.

The Power of Delegation

According to Roberts (1990), every rider who plans to get back on a horse after dismounting requires a horse holder. In his text, *Leadership Secrets of Attila the Hun*, Roberts notes that even Attila would have failed in his conquest without the ability to find loyal chieftains to whom he could delegate national unifications responsibilities for his growing force. Delegation is the process by which responsibility and authority for performing tasks (functions, activities, or decisions) is assigned to individuals.

Delegation involves assigning tasks, determining expected results, and granting authority to the individual to accomplish these tasks. It means conveying *rights* and *obligations* to a subordinate. Delegation includes stating the ends to be achieved and providing the means (authority) to the subordinate to achieve these ends. It is not the same as direction which is telling someone specifically what to do. Delegation is perhaps the most difficult leadership skill for nurses to acquire. Student nurses learn clinical skills by giving direct patient care to small groups of patients but few undergraduate programs provide actual leadership experiences.

Concepts related to delegation include responsibility and accountability.

Responsibility means that the subordinate has an obligation to carry out the activities needed to accomplish the assigned task. *Accountability* is being held answerable for the results. The nurse manager may delegate tasks to another individual, but the manager is still accountable for the performance of these tasks; accountability for delegated tasks cannot be relinquished.

No manager is an island; it takes the work of a team of people-all working toward common goals-for an organization to achieve great things. Despite the urge to try to do everything in an organization, effective managers know they can achieve far more-faster and more efficiently-by assigning specific tasks to their employees by delegation.

I accomplish most of what I do through delegation ---either to time or to other people. If I delegate to time, I think of *efficiency*. If I delegate to other people, I think of *effectiveness*.

Many people refuse to delegate to other people because they feel it takes too much time and effort and they could do the job better themselves. But effectively delegating to others is perhaps the single most powerful high-leverage activity there is.

Transferring responsibility to other skilled and trained people enables you to give your energies to other high-leverage activities. Delegation means growth, both for individuals and for organizations. The late J.C. Penney was quoted as saying that the wisest decision he ever made was to "let go" after realizing that he couldn't do it all by himself any longer. That decision, made long ago, enabled the development and growth of hundreds of stores and thousands of people.

Delegation involves other people. It is one of the principles of personal management. The ability to delegate to others is the main difference between the role of manager and independent producer.

A producer does whatever is necessary to accomplish desired results, to get the golden eggs. A parent who washes the dishes, an architect who draws up blueprints, or a secretary who types correspondence is a producer. A producer can invest one hour of effort and produce one unit of results, assuming no loss of efficiency.

But when a person sets up and works with and through people and systems to produce golden eggs, that person becomes a manager in the interdependent sense. A parent who delegates washing the dishes to a child is a manager. An architect who heads a team of other architects is a manager. A secretary who supervises other secretaries and office personnel is an office manager. Management is essentially moving the fulcrum over, and the key to effective management is delegation.

Two Types of Delegation

Gofer Delegation

There are basically two kinds of delegation: "gofer delegation" and "stewardship delegation." Gofer delegation means "Go for this, go for that, do this, do that, and tell me when it's done." Most people who are producers have a gofer delegation paradigm. They roll up their sleeves and get the job done. If they are given a position of supervision or management, they still think like producers. They don't know how to set up a full delegation so that another person is committed to achieve results. Because they are focused on methods, they become responsible for the results.

There are much better ways, more effective ways to delegate to other people. And they are based on a paradigm of appreciation of the self-awareness, the imagination, the conscience, and the free will of other people.

Stewardship Delegation

This is focused on results instead of methods. It gives people a choice of method and makes them responsible for results. It takes more time in the beginning, but it's time well invested. You can move the fulcrum over, you can increase your leverage, through stewardship delegation. Stewardship delegation involves clear, up-front mutual understanding and commitment regarding expectations in five areas:

1. *Desired Results-* Create a clear, mutual understanding of what needs to be accomplished, focusing on *what*, not *how*; *results*, not *methods*. Spend time. Be patient. Visualize the desired result. Have the person see it, describe it, make out a quality statement of what the results will look like, and by when they will be accomplished.

2. *Guidelines-* Identify the parameters within which the individual should operate. These should be as few as possible to avoid methods delegation, but should include any formidable restrictions. You wouldn't want a person to think he had considerable latitude as

long as he accomplished the objectives, only to violate some long-standing traditional practice or value. That kills initiative and sends people back to the gofer's creed: "Just tell me what you want me to do, and I'll do it."

If you know the failure paths of the job, identify them. Be honest and open -- tell a person where the quicksand is and where the wild animals are. You don't want to have to reinvent the wheel every day. Let people learn from your mistakes or the mistakes of others. Point out the potential failure paths, what not to do, but don't tell them what to do. Keep the responsibility for results with them -- to do whatever is necessary within the guidelines.

3. *Resources-* Identify the human, financial, technical, or organizational resources the person can draw on to accomplish the desired results.

4. *Accountability-* Set up the standards of performance that will be used in evaluating the results and the specific times when reporting and evaluating will take place.

5. *Consequences-* Specify what will happen, both good and bad, as a result of the evaluation. This could include such things as financial rewards, psychic rewards, different job assignments, and natural consequences tied into the overall mission of an organization.

Trust is the highest form of human motivation. It brings out the very best in people. But it takes time and patience, and it doesn't preclude the necessity to train and develop people so that their competency can rise to the level of that trust.

I am convinced that if stewardship delegation is done correctly, both parties will benefit and ultimately much more work will get done in much less time. I believe that a family that is well organized, whose time has been spent effectively delegating on a one-on-one basis, can organize the work so that everyone can do everything in about an hour a day. But that takes the internal capacity to want to manage, not just to produce. The focus is on effectiveness, not efficiency.

Certainly you can pick up that room better than a child, but the key is that you want to empower the child to do it. It takes time. You have to get involved in the training and development. It takes time, but how valuable that time is downstream! It saves you so much in the long run.

This approach involves an entirely new paradigm of delegation. In effect, it changes the nature of the relationship: The steward becomes his own boss, governed by a conscience that contains the commitment to agree upon desired results. But it also releases his creative energies toward doing whatever is necessary in harmony with correct principles to achieve those desired results.

The principles involved in stewardship delegation are correct and applicable to any kind of person or situation. With immature people, you specify fewer desired results and more guidelines, identify more resources, conduct more frequent accountability interviews, and apply more immediate consequences. With more mature people, you have more challenging desired results, fewer guidelines, less frequent accountability, and less measurable but more discernable criteria.

Effective delegation is perhaps the best indicator of effective management simply because it is so basic to both personal and organizational growth.

Stages in Delegation Process

The five stages in the delegation process are (1) analyzing the delegator's job to determine what could be delegated, (2) analyzing the subordinate's job strengths and weaknesses to determine which tasks could be delegated to the subordinate, (3) determining the specific tasks to be delegated and the authority and level of delegation, (4) delegating appropriate tasks to the subordinate, and (5) providing feedback to subordinates and following up to see if the tasks have been accomplished.

STEP 1.

When analyzing their job and the activities that need to be performed, nurse managers should determine which responsibilities can be or should be delegated to others. In addition, personal characteristics that prevent the manager from delegating should be analyzed. Many attitudes -- some valid, and some not -- can lead to under-delegation. The risk factors, time constraints, feelings about subordinates' capabilities, and a strong need to prove oneself are some of the attitudes commonly expressed by managers to explain why they do not delegate more. Poteet (1984) identifies the following obstacles to delegation:

1. Ignorance about the delegation process
2. Incomplete transition from staff to manager
3. Anxiety over prospect of losing technical competence
4. Fear of losing control
5. Crisis management orientation
6. Failure to set goals and timetables
7. Job confusion
8. Desire to control upward communication
9. Competition for managerial positions
10. Personal job insecurity
11. Poor time management
12. Lack of commitment to employee development process
13. Lack of confidence in subordinate's abilities
14. Fear of managerial incompetence

STEP 2.

The second step in the delegation process is to analyze subordinates' jobs to see how much time is available for them to perform delegated tasks, evaluating their capability to perform some of the manager's tasks, and determining the subordinates' characteristics that prevent them from accepting responsibility. These forces include the following, identified by Newman (1956):

1. It is easier to ask the supervisor.
2. Subordinates fear criticism.
3. Subordinates lack information and/or resources to perform the task.
4. Subordinates have more work than they have time to do.
5. Subordinates lack self-confidence.

6.   Positive incentives are inadequate to ensure task performance.

STEP 3.

Step three is deciding what tasks or responsibilities should be delegated and how much authority should be given to the subordinate to achieve these tasks.

Just as a supervisor cannot do everything that must be done, so many functions and activities cannot be delegated. Responsibilities for managers vary from one institution to another, but some responsibilities should never be delegated. These include disciplining an immediate subordinate, handling morale problems within the unit, and responsibilities for which the supervisor or manager has legal accountability. Additionally, it is a mistake for a manager to consistently delegate less-than-desirable tasks. Managers who fail to roll up their sleeves and participate in care generally are not well respected. The staff to whom such managers delegate perceive the him or her as "too good" to become involved. In contrast, nursing supervisors who make a point of answering patient call lights and assisting with direct patient care as needed are more likely to be viewed by the nursing staff as a member and leader of the team. (Sullivan, et al. 1992, pp. 217, 218).

When authority is delegated, two decisions must be made. First, what areas of authority, or what resources, must be person control to achieve the expected results? Second, what are the limits, boundaries, or parameters for each area of authority or resource to be used? A unit manager who is responsible for maintaining adequate supplies needs budget authority. The authority to spend money on supplies, however, may be limited to a specific amount for specific supplies or may be allocated to supplies in general.

In addition, each task that is delegated has a level of responsibility attached to it; thus the manager must provide the subordinate with clear guidelines on how much responsibility he or she has. According to Whetten and Cameron (1984), the five levels of task delegation are:

1.   Gather information for the manager so he or she can decide what needs to be done.

2. Determine alternative courses of action from which the manager may choose.
3. Perform one part of the task at a time after obtaining approval for each new step.
4. Outline an entire course of action for accomplishing the whole task and have it approved.
5. Perform the whole task using any preferred method and report only results.

STEP 4.

This step requires an understanding of the communication process and how tasks should be assigned. If the subordinate lacks the knowledge or ability to perform a task, then he or she must receive training and/or coaching. Key behaviors in delegating tasks include:

1. Give attention to the person.
2. Maintain appropriate nonverbal behaviors -- use open body language, be straight and square to the person, lean toward her, and maintain eye contact.
3. Use an "I" statement to request, such as "I would like…"
4. Explain the specific task to be delegated, the level of delegation, the amount of authority, and the expected completion time.
5. Explain briefly why the task is important.
6. Ask for suggestions.
7. Provide the subordinate with any additional information or resources that might be needed.
8. Ask the subordinate to confirm his or her understanding of the task, the level and authority to be delegated, and the completion time (get feedback).
9. Obtain agreement to do the task.

STEP 5.

The purpose of this step is to provide a feedback and control system to ensure that the delegated tasks are carried out. Decide if written reports are necessary or if brief oral reports are sufficient. If written reports are required, indicate whether tables, charts, or other graphics are necessary. Be specific about reporting times. Identify critical events or milestones that might be reached and brought to the manager's attention. The manager has to decide how closely the assignment will be supervised. However, controls should never be so tight that they limit subordinates' opportunity to grow. Control should be thought through when objectives are established, not as an afterthought. For example, a nurse is responsible for administering medications and therefore is given authority to access drugs, draw up medications, and administer doses to patients. The nurse is held accountable by several controls which might include the narcotics key control, end-of-shift drug counts, review of patients' records, medication charts, and shift reports.

Figure 6.1 shows the primary purpose or goal of supervisory leadership provided by administrators is to promote greater productivity. (Marks et al., *Handbook of Educational Supervision*, 1971, 144). "Whatsoever your hand finds to do, do it with all your might" (Ecclesiastes 9:10). Jesus Himself praised the one who invested his/her talents productively and rebuked the one who buried his/her talent. Productivity is God's business. The task is to preach the gospel to every nook and corner of this earth and then go home to rest. Dictatorial, authoritarian, and even some forms of bureaucratic administration are not the best leadership styles and, in fact, are abhorred by the Lord.

	Primary Purpose of Supervisory Leadership			
	To Facilitate			
GOAL I	Facilitating Development of Goals and Policies Basic to	Teaching		Profitable
GOAL II	Stimulating Development of Appropriate Programs for	and	OR Service OR	
GOAL III	Procuring and Supervising (Managing) Personnel and Materials so as to Implement	Learning		Production
	MAKING THINGS HAPPEN THROUGH THE EFFORTS OF PEOPLE			

Figure 6.1: The primary purposes of supervisory leadership

Principles to Follow in Participation

In their book, *New Dynamic Leadership*, (1994), Bernard and Geeta Lall suggest principles that leaders should keep in mind when making group demographic decisions:

1. Worker participation is a right, privilege, and duty.
2. Because of their specialized qualifications, workers can make valuable contributions (IBM story).
3. Areas to be discussed should be of concern to the workers and the results should be worthwhile.
4. Workers and other participants should be involved in planning the agenda to the best interest of all.
5. Discussion should be kept to the basic purpose, and all decisions should be made within the established frame of reference.
6. Participants should discuss thoroughly and research untiringly before making decisions.
7. The group should be totally responsible for suggested policies.

Despite these principles, some conditions may hamper democratic participation. First, workers who have long worked under authoritarian administration are hard to convince of the merits of democratic participation. Second, the manner of initiation of discussion may determine its success or failure. Finally, it is often hard for an administrator to learn to wait patiently for group action.

Concepts of Organization and Administration

It was once said by an unknown author that a successful leader needs the education of a college president, the executive ability of a financier, the humility of a deacon, the adaptability of a chameleon, the hope of an optimist, the courage of a hero, the wisdom of a serpent, the gentleness of a dove, the patience of Job, the grace of God, and the persistence of the devil.

In *The Age of the Manager Is Over!* Steward Thompson (1975), speaks about management techniques that actually impede performance of organization. What is more striking, according to Thompson, is that executives use these techniques to incapacitate workers of great creative ability.

Thompson says, "The collapse of Penn-Central, of Rolls-Royce, of Atlantic Acceptance, of the Toronto Telegram, of Lockheed, even the whole Watergate scandal of 1972-1973 are instances cited by some to support their argument for more and better management throughout public and private affairs." (Thompson, 1975).

This chapter explores the major functions of a highly effective leader. However, it is important to study the traditional theories of administration and compare these with the contemporary or emerging theories. Times have changed; people have changed. Administrative theories and behaviors have changed also. Therefore, a dynamic leader does not pull new tricks out of the hat like a magician, he/she studies contemporary and emerging theories in light of current research and adapts these to make an organization more productive. In addition, he/she should also study desirable and productive qualities of a dynamic leader as perceived by workers and others.

There are two competing concepts of organization and administration. One is the *traditional concept* of monopolistic and bureaucratic and the other is the *modern concept* of pluralistic and collegial. What are these theories and how do they differ one from the other?

1. *Traditionalist:* Leadership is confined to those holding positions in the power echelon. This premise assumes that people are divided into two groups, the leaders and the followers. The leader has the power to lead. If anyone else tries to assume this leadership role, conflict will rise. If the leader does not assume full leadership and permits others to assume such leadership, his/her own position is threatened.

   Modernist: Leadership is not confined to those holding status positions in the power echelon. Any person is providing leadership when he/she helps a group formulate goals, programs, and policies, helps to attain the group's goals, or helps to maintain the group. The official leader is more effective if he/she develops leadership that is widely dispersed throughout the organization.

2. *Traditionalist*: Good human relations are necessary for followers to accept decisions of super-ordinates. The traditional leader believes that his/her decisions in the power hierarchy must be accepted and implemented or the enterprise will fail. Since supervision and inspection are costly, good human relations are necessary so that subordinates will follow his/her decisions without question.
Modernist: Good human relations are essential to group production and to meet the needs of the individual members of the group. Emerging theories suggest that good human relations improve group morale and productivity. Generally when individual and group needs are met, the organization is more productive.

3. *Traditionalist*: Authority and power can be delegated, but responsibility cannot be shared. Traditionalist have held that authority and power can be delegated to subordinates, but if anything goes wrong, ultimate responsibility lies with the super-ordinate.

Modernist: Quite contrary to the traditional theory, the emergent theorist believes that responsibility, as well as power and authority, can be shared. When potential leaders are given opportunity to exercise their leadership, they will voluntarily accept responsibility as well as authority and power. Since the leader does not have all the responsibility in such situations, he/she should not receive all the credit or all the blame.

4. *Traditionalist*: Final responsibility for all matters is placed on the administrator at the top of the power echelon. For a long time traditionalists have believed that the top executive in an organization is ultimately responsible for everything that happens. He/she receives the credit and the blame. In such a case, he/she has veto power over subordinates' decisions. (It should be apparent, however, that a hospital administrator cannot be held liable for the

malpractice of a physician. The physician is personally responsible for the mistake and is sued.)

Interestingly, in the United Nations Security Council, Russia has cast the largest number of vetoes; perhaps this speaks for itself. If the top executive uses veto power too often, he/she is an outcast.

Modernist: Those affected by a program or policy should share in the decision making with respect to that program or policy. This is beautifully stated in the American Declaration of Independence: "Governments are instituted among men, deriving their just powers from the consent of the governed," Lincoln stated the same thing in the following words: "Government of the people, by the people, for the people." Granted, in large and complex organizations, all members cannot participate directly, but this can be achieved through representation.

5. *Traditionalist:* The individual is secure when super-ordinates protect the interests of subordinates. The top executive should defend subordinates, right or wrong, so long as they are loyal and obedient. This idea is close to feudalism, in which a person serves a lord in return for protection. Subordinates become "rubber stamps in return" for total protection.

Modernist: The individual finds security in a dynamic climate in which he/she shares responsibility for decision making. In the process of implementing goals, policies, and programs, an individual becomes more secure and knowledgeable, and understands these policies and procedures better. He/she is more secure if he/she helps determine personal fate. An effective leader allows democratic decision making that all members of the organization have input.

6. *Traditionalist:* Unity is obtained through loyalty to the administrator. Since the top executive protects subordinates, right or wrong, subordinates own him/her their undivided loyalty. This loyalty requires that subordinates defend themselves and accept the leader's decisions without question. This, too, is an assumption of the feudal system.

Modernist: Unity is secured through consensus and group loyalty. When group members participate in the formulation of goals, policies, and programs, the group is more likely to accept them than if they were handed down through the hierarchy. If the leader works effectively, he/she will be accepted as a group member. Unity is secured through group interaction.

According to Victor Thompson, top executives "are of all people in the organization, the ablest, the most industrious, the most indispensable, the most loyal, the most reliable, the most self-controlled, the most ethical, which is to say the most honest, fair and impartial." (Thompson, 1977).

Unfortunately, even to this day, some leaders hold to the old colonial concept of "divide and rule." This practice has done great harm to organizations. A dynamic manager should know when to be bold and assertive, when to confront problems and deal with them on a personal basis, and when to run the extra mile.

7. *Traditionalist*: Maximum production is attained in a climate of competition and pressure. The traditional assumption is that people excel under pressure and competitive struggles, that success under such circumstances should be rewarded, and that productivity increases in such a climate.

   Modernist: Maximum production is attained in a threat-free climate. By-products of competition and pressure may ultimately reduce production. Although a threat-free climate does not mean a problem-free situation, when workers solve problems together, satisfaction and personal growth increase.

8. *Traditionalist*: The line-and-staff plan of organization should be utilized to formulate goals, policies, and programs, as well as to execute policies and programs. The line-and-staff structure is most competent to formulate goals, policies, and programs. It has responsibility for implementing goals, policies, and programs, and therefore should have responsibility for formulating them.

Modernist: The line-and-staff organization should be used exclusively for dividing labor and implementing policies and programs developed by the total group. Both concepts accept the line-and-staff pattern of organization. The distinct difference is that in the traditional concept, policies are determined and executed by the line-and-staff organization; according to the emerging collegial concept, the administration involves the group in decision making. Emerging theory requires two structures, one to determine goals, policies, and programs and the second to execute such policies and programs.

9. *Traditionalist*: Authority is the right and privilege of a person holding a hierarchical position. The person with the greatest ability should be given vested authority as leader by the board of governors, the state, or the country. Administrators have the greatest ability or they would not have been chosen for the position in the power hierarchy. This assumption can be traced back to the divine-right-of-kings theory.

    Modernist: The situation and not the position determines the right and privilege to exercise authority. Authority arises from the situation rather than from the position. A leader enjoysfargreater authority when he/she derives it because of leadership qualities, expertise, and group respect. One finds himself or herself in a situation wherein one must exercise authority. A teacher assumes authority in a classroom, not because of the position he/she holds in a school system, but because the classroom situation demands that authority.

10. *Traditionalist*: In an organization the individual is expendable. The traditional concept assumes that the goal of the organization is more important than the individual. Therefore, the individual goal should be sacrificed, if necessary, to accomplish the goals of the organization.

    Modernist: The individual in the organization is not expendable. Emerging theorists feel that an organization is established to meet the needs of people in the society. Governments were established to serve people. This does not mean that the organization must perpetuate mediocrity. The organization can be more productive and, in fact, can better achieve its own goals by conserving and improving its members. This can be achieved through self-evaluation, group evaluation, and in-service training.

11. *Traditionalist*: Evaluation is the prerogative of the super-ordinate. It is logical for the super-ordinate to have the responsibility of evaluation. After all, is the leader not responsible for everything? Evaluation provides him/her with opportunities for disciplining employees, keeping the organization trouble-free.

    Modernist: Evaluation is a group responsibility. This, too, appears quite logical when the group participates in the formulation of goals, policies, and procedures. The group knows the criteria or the frame of reference for evaluation and can evaluate more objectively than an individual who may be biased. The process of group evaluation also makes the group more cohesive.

Contrasts Between the Two Concepts

Edgar Morphet, Roe Johns, and Theodore Reller, (1974), point out some basic contrasts between the monopolistic-bureaucratic concept and the pluralistic-collegial concept:

1. The monopolistic-bureaucratic system appears to have a closed climate of human relations as opposed to an open one in the pluralistic-collegial system.
2. The monopolistic concept of administration emphasizes centralized decision making with all authority centered in the super ordinate. Close inspection assures that goals and objectives of the organization are followed; whereas the pluralistic-collegial type of administration encourages participatory decision making and disperses authority throughout the organization. There are two structures for pluralistic

organization. One deals with the hierarchical organization, and the second promotes wider involvement in policy decisions.

3. Communication in the monopolistic structure is vertical. Downward communications are rarely intercepted; upward communication can be intercepted by any number of intermediate administrators.

It is interesting to note, however, that channels of communication in a pluralistic organization are many. It has the vertical, two-way channel, the circular and the horizontal. Strong committee structures provide bottom-line workers with pportunity to communicate face to face with top executives, and the whole structure benefits greatly.

4. Although the monopolistic type of administration is largely authoritarian and the pluralistic type is democratic, it should not be concluded that an authoritarian administration is always bad or a democratic administration is necessarily always good. As a result of a study conducted on school principals at the University of Florida, Morphet et al. (1974) provided the following definitions of democratic and undemocratic behavior:

A.   Democratic Behavior.

(1) Action involving the group in decision making with respect to policy and program.

(2) Implementation in line with democratically determined policy.

(3) Action promoting group or individual creativity, productivity, and satisfaction without harm to other groups or individuals.

(4) Behavior or attitude respecting dignity of individuals or groups.

(5) Action indicating that the administrator seeks to become an accepted member of the group.

(6) Action showing that the administrator seeks to keep channels of communication open.

B. Undemocratic Behavior.

(1) Action signifying that decision making is centered in the status leader or his/her inner circle.

(2) Undemocratic implementation of democratically determined policy.

(3) Action frustrating group or individual creativity, productivity, and satisfaction.

(4) Action indicating that the administrator attains objectives by pressures that jeopardize a person's security.

(5) Action suggesting that the administrator considers himself or herself above or apart from other group.

(6) Action showing that the administrator discourages or blocks free communication.

5. Research studies show that monopolistic-bureaucratic organizations do not appear to be as innovative as the pluralistic-collegial organizations. The monopolistic environment lacks feedback. Morphet et al., (1974) states that "Unless the long-range is built into, and based on short-range plans and decision, the most elaborate long-range plans will be an exercise in futility." He further points out that short-range and long-range planning are based on the time span over which they are effective.

In long-range planning, an organization needs to ask three basic questions:

(1) What should our business be? (2) What is our business? (3) What will our business be? In these three questions is the embodiment of strategic planning. "Everything that is "planned" becomes immediate work and commitment," says Drucker. (p.122). The General Electric Company, according to Drucker, (pp. 123-126), calls this kind of planning "strategic business planning."

PART III
LEADERSHIP AND SKILLS

"The best cosmetic in the world is an active mind that is always finding something new."

-- Mary Meek Atkeson

CHAPTER SEVEN

DEVELOPING COMMUNICATION SKILLS

"Words with me are instruments"
                                        -- Theodore Roosevelt

"Know how to listen, and you will profit even from those who talk badly"
                                        -- Plutarch

The Power of Communication

Norbet Weiner in "The Human Use of Human Beings" says that speech is a joint game between the talker and the listener against the forces of confusion. Unless both make the effort, interpersonal communication is quite hopeless.

Communication is the transmission of information, and information is power because it provides sounder bases for judgments. The informed person is on sounder ground and therefore more powerful. The withholding of information is also a form of power, inasmuch as the person with the information is in a superior position to make decisions. Good and effective communication is sometimes described as active listening, that is, listening with (a) intensity, (b) acceptance, (c) empathy, and (d) a willingness to assume responsibility for understanding the speaker's complete message (Argenti, 1994, p. 25). The barriers that inhibit active listening can be intentional or unintentional, and may be established on either end of the transmission.

Systems of Communication

Organizations are described as having at least two systems of communication existing side by side: the formal and the informal communication processes.

The formal communication process closely resembles the formal organizational structure of hospitals. (Dale, 1978). The administrator may send memoranda to the department managers, or the department managers may send them to their staff.

The informal communication process exists in nearly every organization. The social groups within the institution define the informal communication process (Mintzberg, 1979). Nurses chatting in their lounge communicate informally and exchange much important information in the course of their casual conversation.

Direction of Flow

Communication is the flow of information in the organization, which social scientists describe as flowing upward, downward, and horizontally. As the words themselves suggest, upward communication flows from subordinates upward to the next level(s) of administration. Downward communication flows from upper-level management to lower-level members of the staff. Horizontal communication is information flowing between peers or persons of equal rank or status. (Barnes, 2005).

The closer a person gets to the organizational center of control, the more pronounced the emphasis on the exchange of information. Administrators process information and use it in their decision making. Communicating is at the heart of the management process. It is an art that managers must master. Communications between administrators and personnel are full of subtleties and shades of meaning. Most communication also has numerous levels of meaning and function and is essential to building a relationship. Any act of communication may answer a question at the moment, but it has different meanings for the persons involved. Managers need to be aware that there are many barriers to full, clear communication. Seldom does any single communication have only one level of meaning (Kotter, 1982).

Leadership Personality and Communication

Communication is at the heart of leadership. You must be able to communicate in all directions -- to your subordinates, to your bosses, to your peers both inside and outside your organization, to your customers, and to the public at large. Someone who aspires to leadership and is unable or unwilling to cultivate the ability to communicate is in the wrong line of work (Barnes, 2005, p. 62).

Four forms of communication are writing, speaking, reading, and listening. All the hours we spend doing at least one of those four things. The ability to do them well is absolutely critical to leadership effectiveness.

Communication is the most important skill in life. We spend most of our waking hours communicating. You have spent years learning how to read and write, years learning how to speak. But what about listening? What training or education have you had that enables you to listen so that you really, deeply understand another human being from that individual's own frame of reference? Comparatively few people have had any training in listening at all. (Covey, 1990, p. 237).

Listening

Listening involves a more sophisticated mental process than hearing. It demands energy and discipline. It is a learned skill and the first step is to realize that effective listening is an active, not a passive process. A skilled listener does not jut sit there and allow listening to happen. What then is listening?

Listening is (a) taking in information from speakers, other people or ourselves, while remaining nonjudgmental and emphatic; (b) acknowledging the talker in a way that invites the communication to continue; and (c) providing limited, but encouraging, input to the talker's response, carrying the person's idea one step forward. (Burley, 1995).

Jay Gellert, CEO, Heakthnet, Inc., Woodland Hills, CA once said that "The true leader is always listening. Listening and being truly open to the world around him." Charles M. Cawley, Chairman and CEO, MBNA America, Wilmington, DE also said that "leadership has less to do with walking in front and leading the way than it does with listening to the needs of the people of the company and meeting them."

In his book, *The 7 Habits of Highly Effective People*, Dr. Stephen Covey, (1990), asserts technique called "active and emphatic listening." This is where you paraphrase the speaker's words to ensure that you both fully understand the intent of the dialogue. Keeping your attention on your intention is very crucial to be an effective leader. Of all the things that you may become in life, becoming a good listener is among the most important. The process itself is simple and consists of paying attention and asking question.

Paying attention involves letting the speaker know you're sincerely interested. Make eye contact and maintain it; do not gaze off into the distance or down at the ground. In your peripheral vision, make a note of the person's body language. Focus primarily on the speaker's words with your own words or gestures, but feel free to offer an occasional head nod, an affirming what they are saying.

Asking questions involves letting the speaker know that you really are interested and have been paying attention. This allows the speaker withhold nothing once he sees that your interest is genuine. It also allows you to gently lead the conversation in a new and interesting direction. Moreover, asking questions gives you the opportunity to become more knowledgeable about the particular subject at hand. Asking questions is a good idea whenever you are stuck for a question and enables you to pull out the most effective and reliable standby.

Dr. Stephen Covey continues by saying that when another person speaks, we're usually "listening" at one of four levels. We may be ignoring another person, not really listening at all. We may practice pretending. We may practice selective listening, hearing only certain parts of the conversation. We often do this when we're listening to the constant chatter of a preschool child. Or we may even practice attentive listening, paying attention and focusing energy on the words that are being said. But few of us ever practice the fifth level, the highest form of listening, *empathic listening.*

Levels of Listening

According to Stephen Covey (1990), empathic listening involves much more than registering, reflecting, or even understanding the words that are said. Communications experts estimate, in fact, that only 10 percent of our communication is represented by the words we say. Another 30 percent is represented by our sounds, and 60 percent by our body language. In empathic listening, you listen with your ears, but you also, and more importantly, listen with your eyes and with your heart. You listen for feeling, for meaning. You listen for behavior. You see your right brain as well as your left. You sense, you intuit, you feel.

Because we listen autobiographically, Dr. Covey says we tend to respond in one of four ways. We evaluate – we either agree or disagree; we probe – we ask questions from our own frame of reference; we advise – we give counsel based on our own experience; or we interpret – we try to figure people out, to explain their motives, their behavior, based on our own motives and behavior.

The skills of emphatic listening according to him involve four developmental levels.

The first and least effective is to *mimic content*. This is the skill taught in "active" or "reflective" listening. Without the character and relationship base, it is often insulting to people and causes them to close up. It is, however, a first stage skill because it at least causes you to listen to what's being said. Listening in spurts. Tuning in and tuning out, being somewhat aware of others, but mainly paying attention to oneself. One follows the discussion only enough to get a chance to talk. This is more passive and attention is being faked.

The second level of empathetic listening is to *rephrase the content*. It's a little more effective, but it's still limited to the verbal communication. Hearing words, but not really listening. At this level, people stay at the surface of the communication and do not understand the deeper meanings of what is being said. They try to hear what the speaker is saying but make little effort to understand the speaker's intent. Listeners listen logically, more concerned about content than feeling but remained emotionally detached from the conversation.

The third level brings your right brain into operation. You *reflect feeling*. You are not paying much attention to what he is saying as to how he feels about what he's saying. The fourth stage includes both the second and the third. You *rephrase the content and reflect the feeling.* Listeners refrain from judging the talker and place themselves in the other's position, attempting to see things from his or her point of view. Listener is more concerned about the speaker's feelings and thoughts while suspending one's own thoughts and feeling to give attention solely to listening.

As you authentically seek to understand, as you rephrase content and reflect feeling, you give him psychological air. You also help him work through his own thoughts and feelings. As he grows in his confidence of your sincere desire to really listen and understand, the barrier between what's going on inside him and what's actually being communicated to you disappears. It opens a soul to soul flow. He's not thinking and feeling one thing and communicating another. He begins to trust you with his innermost tender feelings and thoughts.

Empathetic listening takes time, but it doesn't take anywhere near a much time as it takes to back up and correct misunderstandings when you're already miles down the road, to redo, to live with unexpressed and unsolved problems, to deal with the results of not giving people psychological air.

A discerning empathetic listener can read what's happening down deep fast, and can show such acceptance, such understanding, that other people feel safe to open up layer after layer until they get to that soft inner core where the problem really lies. People want to be understood.

Each level overlaps or interchange depending on what is happening. As we move from level 1 to level 3, our potential for understanding, retention, and effective communication increases. All of us listen at different levels of efficiency throughout the day, depending on the circumstances and the people involved. Most of us listen at all three levels during the course of a day. However, the goal is to listen at level 3 in all situations. (Burley, 1995).

In business, you can set up one-on-one time with your employees. Listen to them, understand them. Set up human resource accounting or stakeholder information systems in your business to get honest, accurate feedback at every level: from customers, suppliers, and employees. Make the human element as important as the financial or the technical element. You save tremendous amounts of time, energy, and money when you tap into the human resources of a business at every level. When you listen, you learn. And you also give the people who work for you and with you psychological air. You inspire loyalty that goes well beyond the eight-to-five physical demands of the job.

Before the problems come up, before you try to evaluate and prescribe, before you try to present your own ideas -- *seek to understand.* It's powerful habit of effective interdependence. When we really, deeply understand each other, we open the door to creative solutions and third alternatives. Our differences are no longer stumbling blocks to communication and progress. Instead, they become the stepping stones to synergy. When we communicate, we build bridges. We make the connections that enable ideas to flourish and actions to occur. Healthy connections begin with clarity, and last only as long as we continue to invest in them.

Dr. Stephen Covey (1990) went further to say that the next time you communicate with anyone, you can put aside your own autobiography and genuinely seek to understand. Even when people don't want to open up about their problems, you can be empathic. You can sense their hearts, you can sense the hurt, and you can respond to their needs and feelings. You've shown understanding and respect. Don't push; be patient; be respectful. People don't have to open up verbally before you can empathize. You can empathize all the time with their behavior by being discerning and sensitive to their feelings, their state of emotion and their body languages.

Communication is essential for the survival of any social system. The skills of the administrator in communicating what is to be accomplished and the manner in which it is to be carried out have much to do with the success of the administration in achieving the plan for the facility. Unless the plans of action are successfully communicated to the staff, the plans will, at worst, not be implemented at all, or at best, only partially carried out.

Steps in the communication process are that: (a) someone initiates it; (b) it is transmitted from its source to its destination; and (c) it has an impact on the recipient. Unless and/or until a communication has made its intended impact on the recipient, it has, for all intents and purposes, not taken place.

Listening to Nonverbal

Much is communicated that is not verbal. Even when an employee is not talking, he is still communicating in some manner. One of the most important skills of effective listening is listening to nonverbal of body language such as facial expressions, posture, gestures and eye contact.

Close observation will reveal how much people convey through facial expressions. Watch face color and how it changes as people talk about things they have feelings about. Movements of the lips, mouth, cheek muscles, and eyebrows can provide illuminating data about what is going on internally with the person you are listening to. Be aware of expressions that convey tension, doubt, trust, inattention, and so forth.

A leader who is a skilled listener hears emotional tone of a talker and is aware of feelings not expressed verbally. The tone of voice can convey attitudes that can be a clue about how to deal with a person in a difficult situation. It is important to know that the nonverbal aspect of the communication process is largely unconscious and less likely to be manipulated or disguised by the individual. (Burley, 1995)

Barriers to Communication

The real key to any manager's influence is manager's example, his/her actual conduct. Leader's example flows naturally out of his/her character, or the kind of person his/her truly is -- not what others say the supervisor is or what the supervisor may want staff to think he or she is. It is evident in how staff actually experience the manager.

Administrator's character is constantly radiating, communicating. From it, in the long run, staff members come to instinctively trust or distrust their boss and his/her efforts with them. If the leader's life runs hot and cold, if he or she is both caustic and kind, and, above all, if his or her private performance doesn't square with his or her public performance, it's very hard for staff to open up with. Then, as much as staff may want and even need to receive manager's love and influence, staff may not feel safe enough to expose their opinions and experiences and their tender feelings. Unless staff open up with their supervisor, unless he or she understand them and their unique situation and feelings, manager will not how to advise or counsel them.

Unless leadership is influenced by staff uniqueness, they are not going to be influenced by his or her advice. If you want to be really effective in the habit of interpersonal communication, you cannot do it with technique alone. You have to build the skills of emphatic listening on a base of character that inspires openness and trust. (Covey, 1990, 238).

Agenda Carrying. Each person carries his or her own agenda into every communication situation, preoccupied with his or her own concerns and life experiences. Each individual filters what is communicated by means of his or her own perceptions.

Selective Hearing. Persons hear selectively; that is, they tend to hear what they want to hear, thereby filtering out the unpleasant. A nursing supervisor may wish to communicate to an aide dissatisfaction with one aspect of the aide's performance. To soften the effect, the supervisor may first praise the employee for some other work. The employee may hear the praise and effectively screen out the criticism.

Differences in Knowledge Levels. Persons who have only sketchy knowledge about a topic may process information quite differently from persons who may be more knowledgeable. That is, degrees of sophistication vary among listeners and the "information" they process from a single communication may differ significantly.

The Filter Effect. The manager may be told what the employees believe he or she wants to hear. It is not easy to give bad news to a superior when one already knows such news is not welcome. Ancient Greek literature recounts how frequently the messenger bringing bad news to the king was killed. The implications of this reaction have not been lost on most organizational members.

It seems that no matter how much middle-and upper-level administrators insist they want to hear bad as well as good news, the employees filter the information toward the known bias of the next level of management. When there are several layers of management through which unwelcome news must filter, the upper management may receive little accurate information.

Subgroup Allegiance. Each one of the subgroups in the organization demands allegiance from its members. Tangible and intangible rewards are given in each group, so when a communication arrives, it is interpreted in light of the goals and needs of each subgroup and usually not from the viewpoint of the organization as a whole.

Jay Jackson, in *"The Organization and Its Communication Problems"* (1960) drew the following conclusions:

* People communicate far more with members of their own subgroup than with any other persons.
* People prefer to communicate with someone of higher status than themselves.
* People try to avoid having communication with those lower in status than themselves.
* People will communicate with those who will help them achieve their goals - higher status persons have power to create either gratifying or depriving experiences.
* People communicate with those who can make them feel more secure and avoid those who make them anxious.

Status Distance. The health care facility staff, for example, comprised of a broad range of professional and nonprofessional groups. At the top of the status ladder is the physician on whose orders the majority of the facility activities depend. Numerous health professionals at the middle level are present in the facility: nurses; physical, occupational, and recreational therapists; dieticians; pharmacists; physician assistants, and others. Toward the lower end of the status ladder are the nurses' aides and housekeepers, few of whom have any formal training. It is difficult for lower-level employees to communicate upward. The administrator must be aware of the status sensitivities of these many groups and be capable of successfully fostering the needed communication among all of them.

Language Barrier. Doctors and nurses speak "medically." The pharmacists speak yet another language, the physical therapists have their own jargon. In short, given the great variety of professional specialists who must by regulation be employed or retained as consultants, the health care administrator and the staff who deal with them have an especially difficult task in assuring that quality service is not compromised through miscommunication among these occupations.

Self-Protection. Persons often fail to communicate information that might reflect badly on them, their friends, or the organization. (Translated into the language of practicality, this means the administrator should assure him/herself that the accident report portrays what actually occurred.)

Information Overload. The abundance of information flowing in the facility (as many as 40 to 100 separate forms) may produce an information overload that results in the staff's compromised ability to distinguish among communications requiring prioritizing and those demanding immediate attention.

Others. The administrator must bear in mind that all communication is multidimensional, needing appropriate interpretation to be of use. In sending out a memorandum to employees or engaging in any communication, the administrator must take into account that its effect depends at least on the following:

* feelings and attitudes of the parties toward each other.
* expectations.
* how well the subordinate's needs are being met by the organization- if the facility is supportive, the employee receiving administrative communications may be less defensive and more problem oriented, that is, readier to absorb the communication and comply with the organization's request.

Effective communication of mission involves a lot more than choosing the right words. The right words certainly help, but they are best served when used in conjunction with a well established method.

As a leader, strive to incorporate some of these concepts of communication to provide firm foundation from which to speak, write, or otherwise communicate your message.

Be *clear* in speaking or in writing. To avoid assumptions, your directives, directions, instructions, regulations, and interpretations should be stated as clearly as possible. Leave no stone unturned by asking if anyone has any questions.

Be *concise*. Do not digress from the subject matter and do not waste your listener's time. No one likes to listen to someone rambling on and on.

Be *consistent*. Make up your mind, make a choice, and make the message consistent to all parties at all times. People like to follow a leader who walks the talk time after time. Even when you are wrong and criticized, you make correction. Without criticism, there is little chance for growth.

Be *credible*. Make sure your message is real. When you are joking, let people know.

Be *courteous*. Be friendly. Those simple words and phrases like "Please," "Thank you," "May I," "I'm sorry," are probably some of the most important, simplest, and effective in English language. It does not take much effort to be courteous and to demonstrate respect throughout the course of the day to everyone you encounter. Since people react to good manners with complementary good thoughts and feelings, the greatest value of courtesy is that it naturally commands respect in return.

Be *current*. Speak in the present moment. Keep your people abreast of current developments in order for them to feel empowered and engaged.

Characteristics of a Good Listener

Several research studies have been done at the University of Minnesota identifying several common attributes of effective listeners. The summary of the findings are that:

Good or effective listeners looked for an area of interest in the speaker's message; they view it as an opportunity to gather new and useful information. Effective listeners are aware of their personal biases and are better able to avoid making automatic judgments about the speaker and to avoid being influenced by emotion-charged words. They also tend to listen to ideas, rather than specific facts in a message. Effective listeners keep an open mind.

They listen for new ideas everywhere, integrating what they listen to with what they already know. They are aware and thus listen to others with their total being. They listen from the heart to help stay nonjudgmental. They maintain conscious perspective on what is occurring, rather than remaining unconscious and missing important details. They look for ideas and new ways of doing things, and listen to the essence of things.

Good listeners are not willing to blindly follow the crowd. They are aware that no two people listen in the same way. They stay mentally alert by outlining, clarifying, approving, and adding illustrations of their own. They are introspective and have the capacity and desire to critically examine, understand, and attempt to transform some of their values, attitudes, and relationships within themselves and others. Lastly, they focus their attention on the talker's ideas while listening with feeling and intuition.

CHAPTER EIGHT

DEVELOPING EFFECTIVE ORGANIZATIONAL GOALS AND POLICIES

"Things which matter most must never be at the mercy of things which matter least."

--Goethe

"The most important thing in life is to decide what's most important"

--Jack Cunningham

Managers who set goals in any organization -- compared to those who do not -- accomplish something significant because they know that goals provide direction. Goals tell you how far you've traveled. Goals help to make your overall vision attainable and goals give people something to strive for.

It's one thing to set goals and it's another to achieve them. The best way to ensure that your goals (and your employees' goals) are achieved. According to Nelson and Economy, (2005), goals should be made *'SMART'*: **S**pecific - goals must be clear and concise if you expect your employees to achieve them; **M**easurable - if you can't measure progress toward achieving a goal, you'll never know whether you or your employees have attained them; **A**ttainable - while it's always good to stretch a little to achieve a goal, it should never be unattainable or unrealistic; **R**elevant - employee goals should directly relate to attaining department or organizational goals; **T**ime bond - every goal should have a defined period of time for completion.

Management By Values

In their book, *Managing by Values*, (1997), Ken Blanchard and Michael O'Connor, showed that a Fortunate 500 organization depends on four pillars with acronym 'CEOS'. Each pillar represents a certain group of people to whom the company has a key responsibility. Every person associated with a Fortunate 500 organization, regardless of his or her position, needs to think, feel, and act like a leader.

The letter 'C' stands for 'Customers.' According to them, the first thing that makes a Fortunate 500 organization different is the quality of service available to its customers. To be competitive today is to satisfy your customers and make them brag about you.

The letter 'E' stands for 'Employees.' This is the quality of life available to its employees by creating a motivating environment for its people -- one in which employees can see that working toward the organization's goals is in their best interest. The employees begin to think like company owners.

The letter 'O' stands for 'Owners,' such as stockholders. A company is fortunate when it is profitable. True profit is to be ethical. To be ethical is to maintain integrity -- the trait most cited as required for effective leadership.

The last letter 'S' stands for 'Significant Other.' This includes community, creditors, suppliers, vendors, distributors, or competitors. To be successful is to build a spirit of shared responsibility and mutual trust between your organization and its 'significant others.'"

According to Blanchard and O'Connor, (1997), "the basis for these effective 'CEOS' is 'Managing By Values.'" "It is an accepted business practice for motivating customers to keep coming back, inspiring employees to be their best every day, enabling owners to be both profitable and proud, and encouraging significant others to support their business commitments with you."

Management by values (MBV) process involves clarifying your mission or purpose and values. In a company that truly manages by its values, there is only one boss and that is the company's values. Process for clarifying values involves, getting owner's approval of MBV process. CEO to provide own input about the values. Management team to provide input without CEO. CEO and top management team to share and compare. Employee focus groups to provide input. Check with customers and significant others. Synthesize all inputs and present recommended mission or values to board of directors or owners for final approval.

Another MBV process is communicating your mission and values. Make your mission **ethical** by being fair both with customers and in the marketplace. Ensure equitable and fair treatment of employees. Provide complete and accurate information for shareholders. And provide leadership and practice your values in the community. To be **responsive** is to identify customer expectations and deliver on commitments in a timely manner. Demonstrate respect for all employees and their ideas. Deliver on commitments to shareholders and encourage employee participation in community service. To be **profitable** is to provide cost-effective, technologically superior products for customers. Encourage personal initiative and opportunity for employees. Produce a reasonable return in equity for shareholders and make contributions that strengthen the community.

The last MBV process is aligning individuals, team, and organizational daily practices with your mission and values. "Alignment is the heart and soul of the Managing By Values journey. Once you've clarified your mission and values and communicated them to all your key stakeholders, then it's time to focus on organizational practices and behavior to ensure they're consistent with your stated intentions, priorities, and related performance goals." (Blanchard & O'Connor, 1997).

Webster's New Collegiate Dictionary defines policy as "prudence or wisdom in the management of affairs ... a definite course or method of action selected from among alternatives and in light of given conditions to guide and determine present and future decisions."

Richard Plunkett defines policy as ... broad guidelines for management action formulated by members of top management. They are an effort in coordinating and promoting uniformity in the conduct of the business and behavior of employees. In a corporation, the board of directors would formulate policies which are plans for the promotion of harmony (Plunkett, 1997).

Basically, policy is a broad general statement that primarily guides thinking, decision making, and to some extent, action governing activities required to accomplish a goal. Policy is what an institution, organization, agency, or government chooses to do or not to do. Policy can be written, formally, but many policies are unwritten, unclear, or hidden to prevent public or legal review. Either way, policy should include all actions of an institution, organization, agency, or government.

Procedures, on the other hand, are methods of carrying out individual employee programs and handling day-to-day functions of the organization. In other words, procedure is a step-by-step guide to action that spells out how activities will be carried out in order to attain a goal.

Making Policies and Procedures

Policy making involves and identifies four major stages or processes: formulation, adoption, implementation, and evaluation. Policy formulation has to do with identifying goals, problems, and potential solutions. Policy adoption refers to the authorized selection and specification of means to achieve goals, resolve problems, or both. Implementation follows adoption and occurs when the policy is put to use. Policy evaluation means comparing policy outcomes or effects with the intended or desired effects. (Spradley, 1990).

The ultimate goal of the administrator is to design a program in which every member of the organization makes the same decisions given the same set of circumstances. The purpose and function of these policies is to communicate to each employee as exactly as possible what the management expects in any situation on the job. (Allen, 1997).

It is, of course, neither possible nor desirable to establish policies for every conceivable situation. However, a person can provide guidelines or policies that become the framework within which the employee decides what to do in each situation requiring action on behalf of the organization. G.R. Terry, in his book, *Principles of Management* (1969), has defined policy as a verbal, written, or implied overall guide that sets up boundaries supplying the general limits and direction in which managerial action will take place.

Policies are used to help keep decisions within the areas intended by the planners, since they provide for some consistency in what employees decide in particular situations, usually under repetitive conditions.

Policies reveal the facility administrator's intentions with respect to the behavior of employees, patients, and the public. Policies are decided before the need for employee arises.

Writers in the field of management use policies, procedures, and plans of action as terms to indicate movement from generalized statements of intention (policies) to specific spelling out of the method, step by step (procedures), for carrying out those policies or plans of action.

Policies serve as general statements or understanding that guide or channel subordinates' thinking as they make decisions. Policies limit the area within which a decision is to be made and seek to assure that it will be consistent with the overall objectives. Policies tend to decide issues before hand by establishing the framework and scope of the actions.

The decisions made at each level of management establish the framework for decision making at each successfully lower level of management, generally with progressively decreasing discretion. However, each level of management does participate in the policy making process, and policies are made at every level of management. Policy is made by persons at upper, middle and lower levels of management within the health care facility. (Allen, 1997).

The Importance of Policies

Developing policies has many advantages such as facilitating the orientation of staff or members regarding relations between the organization and the community. It facilitates a similar orientation for the new employees. It acquaints the public with the position of the organization. Policy should provide a reasonable guarantee that there will be consistency and continuity in the decisions that are made under it. It informs the president/leadership what to expect from the board of trustees and what the board of trustees may expect from the president/leadership.

Policy should be stated in a broad, general terms, but in terms that are clear enough to allow for executive direction and interpretation. It should reveal the philosophy of the board of trustees or owners for the employee's understanding. It should provide purpose and rationale for the subject about which the policy is being made, how the matter should be carried out, covers situation tat are likely to occur repeatedly. It should be subjected to review by the trustees, with the objective of improvement in accordance with the changing conditions.

Henry Tosi and Stephen Carroll point out that "the formulation of procedures and policies for programmed decisions is an important organizational task, since they have a significant effect on how efficient an organizational operates" (Tosi and Carrol, 262).

Leonard Kazmier (pp.42-48) says that just as objectives are necessary to give direction to individual and group processes, policies provide strategies to attain these objectives. Whether these policies are written down or not, they serve as guidelines -- as a frame of reference in all business activities and decisions made from day to day. Donnelly, Gibson, and Ivancevich, (1971) mention that the principal means used by management to implement plans is policy making, an important phase of planning. They quote from Higginson's *Management Policies*: "Policies are statements -- which reflect the basic objectives of the firm and which provide the guidelines for carrying out action throughout the firm."

Policies are plans, either specific or general, short-term or long-term, concrete or abstract. They show direction for fulfillment of organizational goals, objectives, and purposes. They provide behavioral direction and control for employees.

Koontz, (1970), quoted by Russell Moore, points out that policy is perhaps one of the most misunderstood management tools. This is due to improper use and inconsistencies in decision-making processes of middle-and lower-level managers. In Koontz's own words: "Too often, policies are regarded as 'written on stone,' and the old cliché that 'we do not know why we do it, it is just our policy' is too often true."

The most important function of policy is to help make consistent decisions while leaving room for different decisions to be based on different facts. Thus, policies serve as a framework or as guidelines. They are directly related to delegation of authority. The administration, even though it has authority to make decisions, must have policies to help it keep consistent.

Types of Policies

Various kinds of policies govern various kinds of organizational activities. Policies are made at the organizational level, at the departmental level, and down to the lowest administrative level. Also, some basic policies apply to all.

Basic policies are general and broad and have an overall effect on the organization. They are observed by managers at all levels. Departmental policies are for the exclusive benefit of departmental employees.

General policies are more specific than basic policies. They apply only to the major part of the organization and are generally used by managers at the middle-management level. Kazmier, (pp. 68-70), gives the example of a policy which says that purchasing agents should work with local contractors whenever possible. This would be classified as a general policy.

In the American Management Association's *Management Handbook*, Koontz states that the variety of policies is legion (Moore, ed. 1970, p. 48). Policies have a hierarchy of existence and they arise from the various functions of the organization. Usually, most policies are made at the top-and middle-management level. Some policies, however, are also made at the lower level.

Policies are directly related to a specific function. Receiving paychecks fortnightly is a policy of the finance department, possibly influenced in part by top-management personnel. Policies relate to promotion, appointment, personnel, marketing, public relations, student services, and many more.

Formulating Effective Policies

Many basic policies are formulated by top-level management to provide guidelines for subordinates so that organizational objectives can be achieved. Currently, however, more and more employees or their representatives are becoming involved in the formulation of policies that directly affect them. Many argue against this procedure, saying that policy determination is the prerogative of top-level administrators alone. All should recognize that when employees have a say in policy determination, they become well aware of these policies, understand their implications, and also help to implement them.

According to Daniel Kazt and Robert Kahn, (1978, p.262), policy making is not only the product of deliberate consideration of long-run problems facing the organization. Policy is also created by day-to-day decisions, often on an ad hoc basis and often made by administrators rather than by designated policy makers.

Most policies originate from requests to top administrators. A Middle- or lower-level manager may not know how exactly how to tackle a problem, so he requests help from his super-ordinates. As this request goes upward in the hierarchy, a decision is made which is similar to the British common law. Once precedents develop, they become guides for the future. Some may argue that an administrative action was taken to deal with a special situation, but some employees will think of it as a precedent and expect like treatment in the future.

Some external sources, such as unions, associations, and government, impose many policies upon organizations. Some people may be naïve enough to think that such policies do not affect organizations in the private sector. On the contrary, many governmental policies have been enacted because of tremendous pressure placed upon them by labor unions, associations, and pressure groups. These policies affect all organizations in the public sector or the private. All public and most private organizations have also been heavily influenced by national labor unions and professional organizations in developing policies relative to personnel administration. Policies regarding salaries, fringe benefits, promotion, demotion, dismissal, reprimand, and the like are often dictated by labor unions.

Two methods of policy formulation are typical. The classical one is related to Max Weber's bureaucratic model of organization. The second is related to contemporary concepts of collegiality.

In the Weberian model, people with authority and responsibility in the hierarchy formulate policies, often as individuals and sometimes as a committee, and then impose these policies upon their subordinates.

Weber's Paradigm

What are the characteristics of Weber's bureaucratic model that have affected policies for so long? Note whether these characteristics are found in organizations today.

1. The Principle of Specialization. Regular organizational activities are distributed in fixed ways as official duties. Since organizational

tasks are too complex to be performed by single individuals or a group of individuals with a single set of skills, efficiency is promoted by dividing those tasks into activities which can be assigned easily to specific offices or positions. This division of labor encourages a high degree of specialization which improves performance in two ways:

A. It allows organizations to employ personnel on the basis of technical qualifications.

B. It allows employers to improve their skills by limiting their activities to a narrow range.

Most organizations in the Western world have accepted Weber's principle. Specialization is needed in medicine, education, industry, and commerce. Even a barber claims to be a specialist in a certain style of haircut.

2. The Principle of Graded Authority. Positions are arranged by levels of graded authority, a firmly ordered system of *super-ordination* and *subordination* in which lower officers are supervised by higher officers. Specialization enhances efficiency in specific tasks but creates problems of coordination. Each official is granted requisite authority to control activities of his/her subordinates. Organizations often rigidly adhere to hierarchical principles to the degree that failure to recognize lines of authority is viewed as an immoral organizational behavior.

3. The Principle of Control and Coordination. Management of activities is controlled by general policies and rules which are stable, exhaustive, and learnable. These rules, constitute standards to assure control and coordination, which in turn account for relative uniformity in the performance of tasks. Together with the hierarchical authority structure, rules also provide for continuity of operations, regardless of changes in personnel. Reviewing any policy book quickly reveals that this principle, too, is accepted and widely used today.

4. The Principle of Rationality. As bureaucracy develops, it tries to eliminate from official business all purely personal, irrational, and emotional elements such as love and hatred. The essence of bureaucratic arrangements is rationality. Only by performing impersonally can officials assure rationality in decision making and only thus can they assure equitable treatment for subordinates. Some organizations, in spite of preaching togetherness and democracy, have accepted the principle of rationality and use it widely today.

5. The Principle of Promotion. Employment in a bureaucracy such as an educational organization is based upon technical competence. Promotions are to be determined by seniority, achievement, or both. Tenure is assured, and fixed compensation and retirement provisions are made. Since individuals with specialized skills are employed to perform specialized activities, they must be protected from arbitrary dismissal or denied of promotion on purely personal grounds.*

(* Copyright 1947 by Oxford University Press, New York)

Collegial Model of Policy Formation

The collegial model is comprised of a community of scholars, especially a concept wherein full participation is allowed in all decision making. This is especially true in institutions of higher education in which a true spirit of the community of scholars exists. This concept is spreading to school systems as well as many industries-IBM, for example.

In the collegial model, scholars generally administer their own affairs. Administrators provide for all types of interaction and facilitate deliberations and decision-making endeavors of scholars. Many times administrators have little or no influence upon these scholars. Examples of this model in practice exist in many liberal arts colleges and emerging universities. The concept that scholars should govern their own affairs comes from the notion that professionally competent should know and actually can administer their own work better than hierarchical administrators.

In this model, an administrator is given a term of two to five years. At the end of

this term, the scholars either reappoint him/her or ask him/her to step down so that

another scholar may take over administrative duties. The administrator who survives in a

situation like this has mastered the skill of involving scholars in democratic decision

making for organizational betterment. (Talcott Parsons and M Weber, 1947 & John

Kenneth Galbraith, 1967) were among the first to advocate the need for competence and technical expertise in the leadership role and in the decision-making processes.

Barry Richman and Richard Farmer, (1974, pp. 28-30), point out that the collegial model confuses what ought to be with what the situation really is. This model works best when an organization has (1) sufficient resources, (2) participative and cooperative members, (3) common values and goals, and (4) commitment to institutional goals and objectives.

Despite certain weaknesses, the collegial model has many strengths worthy of consideration. According to W.B. Castetter, (1976, p. 75), these are as follows:

1. It is bases upon the true concept of democracy.
2. It is not only involves the community of scholars but also brings input from student representatives.
3. It provides fair, courteous, and considerate treatment to all personnel and students.
4. t can create and maintain a hospitable environment that respects the dignity and nurtures the optimum development of individual personality.
5. It avoids discrimination against personnel and students because of membership in any religious order, society, or association.
6. It provides safeguards to protect personnel, teachers, or students against arbitrary treatment.
7. It maintains equality of opportunity for current personnel, teachers, or applicants, irrespective of race, religion, or sex.

8. It selects leaders who are tolerant, patient, and fair with the personnel and students.
9. It encourages organizational citizenship, including freedom of expression and participation in system affairs.
10. It furnishes personnel and students with full information on matters affecting their positions, as well as those having to do with system policies.

A third model, known as the political model of decision making, is advocated by

J. V. Baldrige (1971, p. 1-10). It focuses on problems involving goal setting and values rather than on those of maximizing efficiency in goal achievement. The political model takes interest groups and power blocks into consideration, because political elites have a great deal of power over community decisions.

After interviewing administrators, personnel, or scholars from a large number institutions of higher education, M Cohen and J. March (1986) offer the following properties of *organized anarchies* as the latest model: (1) ambiguity of purpose and problematic goals, (2) unclear technology, (3) fluid participation, (4) ambiguity of power, (5) ambiguity of the inability to learn from experience, and (6) ambiguity of success. The researchers question the value of this model and are skeptical of how much meaningful and effective institutional planning it can accomplish.

Guidelines for Effective Policies

Formulating effective policies is not easy. One needs to study carefully the many dimensions and characteristics of policies. Ziegler, cited by Donnelly et al., (pp. 72, 73), offers the following important characteristics for creating effective policies:

1. Flexibility. A policy must strike a reasonable balance between stability and flexibility. Conditions change and policies must change accordingly. On the other hand, some degree of stability must prevail if order and direction are to be achieved. No rigid guidelines exist to specify the exact degree of requisite flexibility; only the judgment of management can determine the balance.

2. Comprehensiveness. A policy must be comprehensive enough to cover any contingency. The degree of comprehensiveness depends upon the scope of action controlled by the policy itself. If the policy is directed toward very narrow ranges of activity, such as hiring policies, it need not be as comprehensive as a policy concerned with public relations.

3. Coordination. A policy must coordinate interrelated subunits. Without coordinative direction provided by policies, each sub-unit is apt to pursue its own goals. The ultimate test of any sub-unit's activity should be its relationship to the policy statement.

4. Ethics. A policy must conform to prevailing canons of ethical behavior. The manager is ultimately responsible for resolution of issues which involve ethical principles. An increasingly complex and interdependent contemporary society has resulted in a great number of ethical problems which are only vaguely understood.

5. Clarity. A policy must be written clearly and logically to specify the aim of the action it governs, define appropriate methods and action, and delineate limits of action.

    The ultimate test of the effectiveness of a policy is whether the intended objective is attained. If the policy does not lead to the goal, it should be revised. Thus, policies must be re-examined continually.

Moore (p. 51) offers the following guidelines in formulating effective policies.

1. Make sure that policies reflect objectives and plans. Since policies are to guide decision making and to give consistent structure to plans, those that do not make the attainment of enterprise objectives more effective and efficient are inadequate.

2. Policies should represent a consistent pattern. An ineffective marketing program would surely result if, for a given product

and market, a company should try simultaneously to support a policy of vigorous price competition and a policy to gain product differentiation by heavy advertising.

3. Policies should be sharply distinguished from rules and procedures. As pointed out previously, where policies are involved, the decision maker is expected to think within his/her limits; but in the case of rules and procedures, the thinking has already been applied.

4. Policies must be looked upon as subject to change. Too often policies are considered unchangeable and sacrosanct. To be sure, a few policies such as those based on common codes of honesty and decency are unchangeable. But most policies, being guides for future action, must remain flexible to future changes.

5. Policies should be in writing. Writing a policy does not necessarily make it clear, but a policy that cannot be put in writing is at best unclear. The difficulty of communicating intentions and desires is reduced by precise writing. Furthermore, the very act of writing policies has a way of eliminating fuzziness and inconsistency.

6. Policies should be taught. No manager may ever assume that even a carefully written policy is always understood. People have a way of putting their own interpretation on any written statement. The effective manager therefore takes every opportunity to teach the meaning of policy: through answering questions, reviewing super-ordinates' decisions, holding staff meetings, and even conversing casually.

7. Policies should be controlled. Policies have a way of being misinterpreted or becoming obsolete. To avoid these possibilities, regular reviews of policies and their application should be made to ascertain whether they are up-to-date, whether they are complete, whether they support or hamper attainment of goals and plans, whether they are understood, whether managers are actually being guided by them in decision making, and whether managers regard them (rightly or wrongly) as interfering with sound action.

Ronald W. Rebore, (1991, pp. 7, 8), concludes that a properly conceived and phrased policy has the following characteristics:

*   It is stated in broad, general terms, but in terms that are clear enough to allow for executive direction and interpretation;
*   It reveals the philosophy for the organization;
*   It provides purpose and rationale for the subject about which a policy is being made;
*   It suggests how the matter is to be carried out;
*   It is never executive in substance or tone;
*   It covers situations that are likely to occur repeatedly;
*   It is always subject to review with the objective of improvement in accordance with changing conditions;
*   (But) it is stable even during personnel changes.

CHAPTER NINE

DECISION MAKING PROCESS

"To govern is to choose."
                                                        -- John F. Kennedy

*"Every human being makes decision daily and deciding
not to make one is also a decision making"*
                                                        -- Author Unknown

Daniel Griffiths comments that "decision making is generally recognized as the heart of organization and the process of administration. (Griffiths, 1969, p. 140).

Hoy and Miskel, (p. 300) express a similar idea: "Decision making ... is the process by which decisions are not only arrived at but implemented. An understanding of the decision-making process is a sine qua non for all administrators. The formal organization is basically a decision-making structure."

The value of a decision depends upon whether it is made under risk conditions, it is a generic situation, an exception to the rule, a policy decision, an administrative decision, or an executive decision. A decision is classified as a judgment -- a choice between alternatives. The alternatives are usually two different courses of action, not always the difference between right and wrong. (Morell, 1969, pp. 251-253).

The purpose is to arrive at the best choice, which may not be as easy as it seems, for there are many elements which constitute effective decision making.

Some decisions may affect a single individual and others may affect a whole group. In each case it is important that it be value-centered, morally sound, and goal oriented.

Characteristics of an Effective Decision Maker

We do not live in an era of intuition. Society, science, technology, and automation demand certain characteristics to better ourselves and successfully fulfill our roles. There are also characteristics of an effective decision maker.

Courage

The people with whom one works, the committee or group, family, and neighbors, all have respect for a man or woman of moral courage.

Webster's New Collegiate Dictionary defines courage as a "mental or moral strength to venture, persevere, or withstand danger, fear, or difficulty."

One aspect of leadership is decision making. If an individual feels uncomfortable making decisions or overwhelmed by anxiety and confusion, then he should not accept leadership because decisions are sometimes painstaking and demand effort and courage. Peter Drucker (page 252) points out that when issues and alternatives have been considered, it is time to act and not time to evade the issue.

Ellen G. White (T3, p. 497) comments that "the cause of God demands men who can see quickly and act instantaneously at the right time and with power. If you wait to measure every perplexity you meet, you will do but little. You will have obstacles and difficulties to encounter at every turn, and you must with firm purpose decide to conquer them, or they will conquer you."

Again she warns in (T3, p. 403), "if a man is divided, undecided, unsettled, until he is sure that he will lose nothing, he shows that he is a man God cannot use. But many are working in this line."

Harry A. Bullis, (1963) retired chairman of the board of General Mills, gives us insight into executive leadership. He comments that lack of courage . . . Excludes many otherwise highly qualified men and women for executive roles. According to a study of unsuccessful executives in more than 200 firms, conducted by the Laboratory of Psychological Studies of the Stevens Institute of Technology, inability to make decisions is one of the principal reasons executives fail. It is a much more common reason than lack of specific knowledge or technical know-how.

Communication

As discussed under the section "Communication", for a committee to obtain a full and enriched discussion, communication is necessary. God has made us capable of communicating, but we sometimes communicate very poorly.

Much success in providing free communication channels lies within the style of leadership. The attitude and behavior of an authoritarian leader who wants to impose his/her will and wants things done his/her way distorts all channels of communication and easily turns off the full cooperation and contribution of its staff members. The culminating point in decision making is when everyone is freely and actively cooperating with his/her ideas. Open communication frees the potential of a group.

As we strive to reach effective decisions, we must remember that everyone on the staff should have representation. Kimball Wiles and John T. Lovell (1975, p. 99), observe that "The critical factor is to provide an easy flow of communication up, down, and sideways."

They give further points for communicating within a discussion committee:

(1) Create an easy yet businesslike atmosphere, (2) guide the flow of the discussion,

(3) clarify questions (4) keep the group on the topic, and (5) summarize the discussion. (pp. 101, 102).

Remember in decision making, the leader is seeking an effective exchange of ideas guided by a common purpose, where utilization of knowledge and ability become important.

Ellen White (T9, p.278) observes that in no conference should propositions be rushed through without time being taken to weigh carefully all sides of the question. Because the president of a conference suggested certain plans, it has sometimes been considered unnecessary to consult the Lord about them. Thus propositions have been accepted that were not for the spiritual benefit of believers and that involved far more than was apparent at the first casual consideration. Such movements are not in the order of God. Many, very many matters have been taken up and carried by vote that have involved far more than was anticipated and far more than those who voted would have been willing to assent to had they taken time to consider the question from all sides.

Urgency vs. Procrastination

Philip Marvin discusses the importance of promptness:

The weight and responsibility which accompanies some decisions require many hours of hard work. Sometimes a wrong decision can definitely mean the loss of a job or mental or physical injury to a loved one. Arriving at sound and healthy decisions isn't always an easy task. But no matter how painstaking a decision may be, it is important to treat it as urgent in order for action to occur. I am not referring to the hasty, non-valid decisions that we are accustomed to making. Rather, I am speaking of those decisions that are difficult to make and require prompt action. The problem is that we have the habit of procrastinating, delaying our decision. Why do it today when we have tomorrow? Some people have developed the art of "passing the buck." People do not want to have the responsibility, so they pass it to someone else. It is very common for an administrator to suddenly be off on a "two-week vacation." His secretary becomes accustomed to saying, "He's not in, and I don't know when he'll be back." "'Deferred' decisions are decisions which have no action. They do not mold the present or the future. The present and the future may take a course of action but not that which you had in mind." (1971, pp. 177,178).

Leadership Roles in Decision Making

Effective decision-making processes have a lot to do with leadership behavior. This cannot be overlooked. Attitude and behavior of a leader have tremendous influence upon group behavior.

Most harmful is the authoritarian style -- one in which subordinates are to accept authority without question. To challenge means punishment of some sort. Human relations are very poor under this system. Workers are always on the defensive, afraid that the master will crack the whip and dismiss someone that leader will use the reward system to motivate his/her subordinates. There is no participation, exchanging of ideas; expertise potential is subdued, and people are manipulated to accomplish the leader's goals.

The autocratic approach appears to be a defense mechanism for feelings of insecurity, inferiority, and incompetence. "He feels that his appearance as a tough guy skillfully conceals his doubts, his feelings of uncertainty, and his state of indecision." (Morell, p. 75).

Kimball Wiles and John Lovell (p. 71) summarize research in group dynamics:

It has been found that: A group with a harsh, dominating official leader is characterized by intense competition, lack of acceptance of all members, buck passing, avoidance of responsibility, unwillingness to cooperate, aggression among members and toward persons outside the group, irritability, and a decrease in work when the supervisor is absent. A group with a benevolent autocrat for an official leader loses initiative, shows regression to childlike dependence, become increasingly submissive, does not continue individual development, cannot accept added responsibility easily. A group with an official leader who exerts no leadership is disinterested, indifferent, lacks purpose or goals, obtains no sense of achievement, and fails to produce. A group in which the official leader concentrates his efforts on helping the persons for whom he is responsible to operate as a group is characterized by cooperation, enthusiasm, acceptance of greater responsibility, a sense of importance of work being done, and a recognition among members of the worth of each other. The last of these types of relationships between the official leader and the staff seems to offer the greatest amount of promise for releasing the full power of a staff.

The work of the democratic leader is to develop power within the group. Participation in planning, goal setting and group opinion is the job of the leader. The important issue is not his opinion, but the opinion

141

and consensus of the group. Under this style of leadership, staff morale is increased, motivation of personnel does not become a problem and the final outcome may be that of productivity and goal reaching. (pp. 71, 39).

Group Decision Making

Today's management practices are oriented toward group decisions. The individual's socio-emotional needs are emphasized. Progress is thought of as finding the happy medium where individual needs and society's rules and regulations are met. Society has its own rules and regulations where production must be met. On the other side of the coin, individuality cannot be ignored. People have personal needs -- needs of recognition, esteem and self-worth -- that if trampled upon or abused causes individualism to rise and destroys society. Strikes, riots, and internal wars are only a few signs and results of oppressed individualism. The task of the administrator, executive, or manager is to find the happy medium. Techniques of the group process are outlined below.

Consensus

As individuals discuss issues related to an enterprise, whatever it may be, the group should make decisions on the basis of consensus. It is the issues and ideas that are important. The group votes on what it considers to be important.

One problem is that whenever participants try to "score points" or "win the other person," they do not contribute for the sake of the group consensus, but for the sake of showing people what they know. They want their personal ideas to be enforced rather than those of the group.

Some questions need to be asked: Is it status within the group I am seeking? Am I jealous of others because people do not implement my ideas? Am I impulsive, not really considering what I say before I say it? Am I contributing to the group or to myself? Am I a negative competitor, always on the defensive side? If so, why?

Meetings of any kind are not places to win approval for one's own point of view. On the contrary, they are places where people join to contribute expertise so solutions may arise and action take place.

Hampton et al. (1973, p. 333.) observed that competition and cooperation are inferred from measures of groups in which members are operating primarily for personal interest, in contrast with groups in which members are more concerned with group needs. These studies show rather consistently that group members who have been motivated to cooperate show more positive responses to each other, are more favorable in their perceptions, and more involved in the task, and have greater satisfaction with the task.

The important thing is to listen to what others have to say and try to see whether ideas can merge to find the best solution to a given problem. We should achieve consensus in those ideas that show most potential in problem solving. That is, we must work with the group to develop its potential in order to arrive at sound decisions.

Steps in Decision Making Process

Various management and decision-making authorities have created a process whereby one can best arrive at decisions. Peter Drucker, industrial consultant and author of *Concept of Corporation* and *The New Society*, suggests in his book, *The Practice of Management*, (p. 353-364) five steps to decision making: (1) Define the problem, (2) analyze the problem, (3) develop alternative solutions, (4) decide upon the best solution, and (5) convert the decision into action.

Define the Problem. The leader must take time to really understand the what, who, where, when, and how of the problem. Many times he may consider symptoms of the problem, but not the problem itself. For example, if there is no food in the house, one may conclude that it is because there is no money. Money is merely a symptom. The real problem may be that the workers of the house are sick or unemployed. Therefore, no work results in no money and, consequently, no food.

Gather Data. To decide between alternatives, it is necessary to have as much information as possible. Lack of accurate information can sometimes cause uncertainty, confusion, and misunderstanding. Take advantage of the professional that may be within the group.

Let them contribute. Don't play Mr. Superman, for that only hinders the process of decision making.

Study the Problem Carefully. Keep a picture of the total program in mind. The staff should be informed of details that involve a decision. Where did we come from, and where are we going? Why are we selecting this approach? Take time to consider the problem thoughtfully.

Identify the purpose. Why is a decision necessary? What needs to be determined? State the issue in the broadest possible terms.

Set the Criteria. What needs to be achieved, preserved, and avoided by whatever decision is made? The answers to these questions are the standards by which solutions will be evaluated.

Weigh the Criteria. A simple methodology is presented. Each criterion is ranked on a scale of values from 1 (totally unimportant) to 10 (extremely important).

Consider the Alternatives. List all possible courses of action. Is one alternative more significant than another? Does one alternative have weaknesses on some areas? Can these be overcome? Can two alternatives or features of many alternatives be combined?

Decision making involves judging various alternatives and then taking action. One common problem seems to be the development of alternatives. People tend to work with the extremes. Drucker, (pp. 359 & 350), suggests a "systematic approach."

Benjamin Franklin (pp. 19 & 20) had a rather long but effective procedure for decision making when he said:

My way is to divide half a sheet of paper by a line into two columns, writing over one Pro and over the other Con. Then, during three or four days consideration, I put down under the different heads short hints of the different motives, that at different times occur to me, for or against the measure. When

I have thus gotten them altogether in one view, I endeavor to estimate their respective weights: and where I find two, one on each side, that seem equal, I strike them both out. If I find a reason pro equal to some two reasons con, I strike out the three. If I judge some two reasons con equal to three reasons pro, I strike out the five: and thus proceeding I find at length where the balance lies; and if after a day or two of further consideration, nothing new that is of importance occurs on either side, I come to a determination accordingly. And, though the weight of reasons cannot be taken with the precision of algebraic quantities, yet when each is thus considered, separately and comparatively, and the whole lies before me, I think I can judge better and am less liable to make a rash step; and, in fact, I have found great advantage from this kind of equation in what may be called moral or prudential algebra.

Test Alternatives. First, using the same methodology as in weighing the criteria, rank each alternative on a 10-high scale. Second, multiply the weight of each criteria by the rating of each alternative. Third, add all the scores and compare the results.

Trouble shoot. What could go wrong? How can you plan? Can the choice be improved?

Evaluate the action. Is the solution being implemented? Is it effective? Is it costly?

Satisficing is not a misspelled word; it is a decision-making strategy whereby the individual chooses an alternative that is not ideal but either is good enough (suffices) under existing circumstances to meet minimum standards of acceptance or is the first acceptable alternative.

An optimizing approach, by contrast, first identifies all possible outcomes, examines the probability of each available alternative, and then takes the action that yields the highest probability of achieving the most desirable outcome.

Sullivan et al (1992), says managers who solve problems using satisficing usually lack specific training in problem solving and decision making. They view their departments as drastically simplified models of the real world and are content with this simplification because it allows them to make decisions with relatively simple rules of thumb or from force of habit. Optimizing techniques, however, make demands on their willingness and ability to collect information, analyze it, and choose the best alternatives.

Decision-Making Conditions

The question is often asked whether decision making is an individual or an organizational process: Do managers of organizations make decision? Managerial decision making is treated essentially as an individual process that occurs in an organizational context. Even though decision making is basically individual, the conditions surrounding it can change dramatically. Within the organization, when managers know the alternatives and the conditions surrounding each alternatives, a state of *certainty* is said to exist. In organizational settings few decisions are made under certainty. The complexity of consumer satisfaction problems makes such situations rare.

The more common decision-making condition is that of risk. The manager does not always know the state of the situation. The key element in decision making under conditions of risk is to accurately determine the probabilities of each alternative. Probability is the likelihood, expressed as a percentage, that an event will or will not occur. If something is certain to happen, its probability is 1.00. If it is certain not to happen, its probability is 0. If there is a 50-50 chance, its probability is .50.

Most critical decision making in organizations is done under the condition of uncertainty. The individual making the decision does not know all the alternatives, attendant risks, or likely consequences of each. Uncertainty originates with the complex and dynamic nature of the organization.

Leaders must make decisions all the time -- it's what they do. Different leaders have different approached to reaching decisions. Some leaders like to study short reports with specific recommendations by the key people involved in the area in question and then arrive at a decision on their own.

Others prefer sitting in a room full of advisers, kicking ideas around until a consensus is reached. Still others have one or two highly trusted advisers present when all decisions are made. Some leaders go with their gut reaction to a problem and make decisions on the spot. Many executives delegate decisions - especially the smaller ones -- to others; some executives want to be in on every decision, large and small.

As a leader, you must find a way of making decisions that works for you. You need to be comfortable with your decision-making process, and you should be confident in your final decisions. This doesn't mean that you can never be wrong, just that you should feel you have made the right decision based on the factors as you knew them at the time. You can't know in advance if a decision will be right or wrong or somewhere in between, but you want to feel that you have done all you can to arrive at the proper decision following the rules and procedure of the organization.

How to Develop Your Own Decision-Making System

1. *Find your style.* Decision making is the essence of what a leader does; some kind of process is essential to carry it out. Your decision making will leave much to be desired if it is haphazard and random. Establish your style; then adapt it to circumstances. No one process is replicable for all executives at all times. Find one that suits your personal style and circumstances.

2. *Get into a routine and learn to pace yourself.* Overwork is a recipe for inattention and mistakes. Determine when you are at your best in contemplating decisions and then try, within reason, to work on your decision making at these optimum times. If you do your best thinking in the morning, for example, you should try not to push yourself to reach a hurried decision toward the end of the workday. Remember, too, that you can mull over decisions while doing other things, such as commuting or working.

3. *Attend fewer meetings.* Most office environments feature too many meetings. Decide which ones are essential and keep them to a minimum. As the leader, you may find that you should step away

and allow some meetings to take place without you. There may be many meetings that will accomplish much more without your presence. Your staff can come up with their recommendations, then pass them on to you for the final decision. Not only does this free up your valuable time, it helps your subordinates grow into their roles as advisers and decision makers.

4. *Go to the source if you need more information.* People are generally flattered when higher-ups call and ask for their specialized knowledge. Find out whom in your organization to go to for the answers to what kinds of questions. Keep in mind that smart, talented people have many fields of expertise, often outside their main responsibility, so take the time to find out what areas your people know. Ted Sorensen was a lawyer with little interest in writing or speaking who was brought in to develop policy positions for young Senator Jack Kennedy. He came to be JFK's trusted speechwriter and one of his closest aides.

5. *Try to get people to speak openly and candidly.* This is frequently difficult to do but is essential to get the information you need to make the right decisions. Your staff should never be afraid to speak their minds in your presence or to deliver information you may not want to hear. You may disagree with them or disregard their advice, but they should always feel free to give it. However, insist that your subordinate be able to back up their statements if you question them beyond their surface recommendation.

CHAPTER TEN

EFFECTIVE STAFF MOTIVATION

"Motivation is what gets you started. Habit is what keeps you going"

-- Anonymous

"To talk about the need for perfection in man is to talk about the need for another species"

-- Author Unknown

A continual and troublesome question facing managers today is why some employees perform better than others. A number of variables have been used to explain performance differences. For example, characteristics such as ability, instinct, and aspiration levels, as well as age, education, and family background explain why some employees perform well and others poorly. Based on these factors, a model that considers motivation and ability as determinants of job performance is presented in Figure 10-1.

Employee Performance	=	f (Motivation	and	Ability)
* Daily job performance		* Compensation		* Recruitment
* Absenteeism		* Benefits		* Selection
* Lateness		* Job design		* Training
* Rule violations		* Supervisory style		* Special programs
* Accidents		* Recruitment and selection		
* Theft				

Sullivan, Eleanor J., Effective Management Nursing, 3rd Edition, © 1992, p 334. Reprinted by Permission of Pearson Education, Inc., Upper Saddle River, NJ.

Figure 10-1 A Simplified Model of Job Performance

Managers spend considerable time making judgments about the fit among individuals, job tasks, and effectiveness. Such judgments are typically influenced by both the manager's and the employee's characteristics. Making decisions about who performs what tasks in a particular manner without first considering individual behavior can lead to irreversible long-term problems. Each employee is different in many respects. A manager needs to ask how such differences influence the behavior and performance of the job requirements. Ideally this assessment is performed when the new employee is hired. In reality, however, many employees are placed in positions without the manager having adequate knowledge of their abilities and/or interests. This often results in problems with employee performance, as well as conflict between employees and managers.

Employee performance literature ultimately reveals two major dimensions as determinants of job performance: motivation and ability (Hershey & Blanchard, 1988). The model presented in figure 10-1 portrays employee performance as a function of these two dimensions (Decker, 1982). This job performance model identifies six performance categories likely to be viewed as important by the manager. Although there is conceptual overlap in these categories, separate designation of each helps emphasize their importance.

The Need to Motivate the Staff

All human behavior is motivated by something; very little human behavior is completely random or instinctive. Most human behavior is goal directed: People do things for some reason, to get a certain result. It is given that employees who are motivated tend to work harder and stay longer with a company. How do we then motivate our employee? According to Townsend et al. (2007), no one can motivate an employee because motivation is internal. It is the job of the supervisors to stimulate the employee's motivating factors.

Recognition is one of the most powerful activities that a manager can do to increase productivity, improve morale, and provide a sense of meaning on the part of employees on a day-to-day basis. Yet, in most work environments, this activity is underutilized and even randomly applied. Studies indicate that being thanked for doing a good job is one of the most motivating incentives an employee reports receiving, even though some 58 percent of employees say they seldom if ever receive such thanks from their managers where they currently work. When recognition is tied to desired performance, it becomes a big driver of enhancing that performance, both the quantity and quality of individual effort and results.

According to Sullivan et al. (1992), an understanding of motivational processes is essential for a more complete understanding of such other factors as leadership, job design, and incentive systems as they relate to employee performance and satisfaction.

What Motivates the Staff?

According to Townsend et al. (2007), supervisor's ability to understand each employee's personal goals serves as the key to motivate employee. Many employees have typical goals to get a good job, good salary, good co-workers, fair supervisors, non-threatening working environment, and to receive timely raise and recognition or rewards they deserve.

However, most managers feel that the only thing that their staff want is more money. While money can be an important way of letting employees know their worth to the organization, it tends not to be a sustaining motivational factor to most individuals. Salary raises are nice, but seldom are they what motivates people to do their best on the job. Effective techniques to keep your employees involved and motivated on an ongoing basis includes

1. Personally thank your staff for doing a good job -- one on one, in writing, or both. Do it timely, often, and with sincerity.

2. Take the time to meet with and listen to employees -- as much as they need or want.

3. Provide your staff with specific and frequent feedback about their performance and support them in improving performance.

4. Recognize, reward, and promote high performers; deal with low and marginal performers so that they improve or leave.

5. Provide information on how the company makes and loses money, upcoming products, services and strategies for competing, and explain their role in the overall plan.

6. Involve staff in decisions, especially those decisions that affect them so they could be more committed.

7. Give staff a chance to grow and develop new skills; encourage them to be their best. Show them how you can help them meet their goals while achieving the organization's goals. This helps to create a partnership with each employee.

8. Provide staff with a sense of ownership in their work and their work environment. This ownership can be symbolic (e.g., business cards for all employees, whether they need them to do their job or not).

9. Strive to create a work environment that is open, trusting, and fun. Encourage new ideas, suggestions, and initiative. Allow them to learn from, rather than being punished for, mistakes.

10. Celebrate successes -- of the company, of the department, and of individuals. Take time for team and morale-building meetings and activities. Be creative, fun, and fresh.

It is important to understand that no single approach to motivating staff members is likely to maximize staff performance and satisfaction. Some methods may work better than others with different people or in different settings. However, each theory of work motivation contributes something to our understanding of and, ultimately, our ability to influence employee motivation. All of the motivational factors can be integrate to some extent by recognizing the need basis of every employee and the goals and the expectancy of the organization as well.

People have needs for money, or at least the things that money can buy, and to some extent they have other needs that can be fulfilled through proper job design, assignment of tasks, social environment, personnel practices such as compensation, promotions, and job security.

The effective management of staff motivation relies upon a combination of approaches, taking into consideration individual needs and job satisfaction. Such an approach is far more likely than any single method or technique to produce effective job performance. The key to effective motivation is really the manager's attitude that it can be done with a little thought and effort. Motivation of staff members is not always easy, but it is certainly one of the most important parts of the manager's job. With practice and a little ingenuity, most managers find that far more can be done than they had initially realized to motivate their staff to high levels of performance.

Staff Motivation and Performance

As stated earlier, motivation describes the forces acting on an employee that initiate and direct behavior. Because individuals bring to the workplace different needs and goals, the type and intensity of motivators vary among employees. Managers prefer motivated employees because they strive to find the best way to perform their jobs. Motivated employees are interested in producing high-quality products or services; they are more likely to be productive than are non-motivated workers. This is one reason that motivation is an important aspect of enhancing employee performance. Figure 12-1 shows staff motivation influenced primarily by the organization's compensation system, benefits program, job design, style of supervision, and methods of recruitment and selection. Having a performance-based compensation/reward system has been demonstrated to have a direct impact on employee motivation. (Sullivan et al.,1992).

Benefits can also influence employee performance and behavior. Most institutions offer their employees paid sick leave. Typically, institutions offer programs that have the following elements: (1) for every X days worked, employees accrue a specific number of paid sick days; (2) there is a maximum number of sick days that an employee can accumulate; (3) notification of the superior is required to be paid for a sick day; and (4) employees who leave the organization without using accumulated sick leave lose these sick days. It is not surprising that these institutions experience relatively high rates of employee absenteeism since there is no reward (motivator) for not using the sick days accumulated. One way to enhance employee performance is to provide options for use of this benefit such as paid time off and/or accumulated vacation time, rather than encouraging employees to "call in sick" to use this benefit.

The number of institutions offering wellness programs or fitness centers for employees has increased significantly in the past two decades. Although few data are available, some evidence suggests that these programs do serve as motivators for the staff (Rhodes & Steers, 1990). In addition, employee assistance programs (as a benefit) recognize that alcohol and substance abuse, as well as psychological problems, are behaviors that often lead to lowered productivity and performance problems (McCafferty, 1988).

Similarly, job enrichment, which is the practice of increasing an individual's discretion to select job activities and outcomes, increases the fulfillment of growth and autonomy needs. This practice increases job depth by providing direct feedback, new learning, participation in scheduling, job uniqueness, control over resources, and an opportunity for employees to be accountable for their jobs (Hershey & Blanchard, 1988).

Managers also can influence the motivation of employees by being sensitive to variations in employee needs, abilities, and goals. The leadership style assumed by the manager reflects a commitment to maximizing each employee's potential. If performance needs to be improved, then managers should intervene to help create an atmosphere that encourages, supports, and sustains improvement. Managers should try to provide employees with jobs that offer equity, task challenge, diversity, and a variety of opportunities for need satisfaction. The manager should also be sensitive to individual differences and consider variations in preferences (valences) for rewards among employees. Employees in one study who were encouraged to participate in practice-related decision making had increased motivation because of this activity (Lawler, 1986). This does not mean all employees benefit from increased participation. In fact, some employees prefer to be followers and have decreased performance when placed in independent roles. (Kelly, 1988).

Providing realistic job information can increase employee satisfaction and reduce employee turnover. When given accurate information about a position, job candidates can "self-select" out of jobs that are not seen as offering opportunities they value. This is especially important in today's job market for health care professionals, since high vacancy rates in certain specialty care areas, such as intensive care units, "force" applicants to accept positions they ordinarily would not consider. Methods of screening are recommended to identify prospective employees who are not likely to be motivated by what a position offers (Gatewood & Field, 1990).

CHAPTER ELEVEN

STAFF DEVELOPMENT

"Let no man imagine that he has no influence. Whoever he may be, and wherever he may be placed, the man who thinks becomes a light and a power"

--Henry George

"The basis of integrity consists, as the great Adam Smith saw so clearly, in the ability to transcend the concept of praise and concern ourselves with the concept of praiseworthiness."

-- Elton Trueblood

It is literally impossible today for any individual to take on a job or enter a profession and remain in it for twenty or more years with his or her skills basically unchanged. Therefore, staff or employee development is not only desirable but also an activity to which each enterprise must commit human and fiscal resources if it is to maintain a skilled and knowledgeable staff.

Employee development typically means training staff members through workshops and in-service trainings to enhance their knowledge and expertise. Enhancing employee knowledge and expertise is an important goal of staff development because it plays a critical role in building internal organizational strengths that an organization needs in a competitive environment.

In every organization, employees have so much to figure out: formal and informal chains of command, the ins and outs of office policies and politics, the right and wrong ways to get the support and resources you need to get your job done. Employees have to learn new skills and techniques to improve the way they do their jobs. All of this requires training, and it requires the attention of the managers who are responsible for ensuring their employees have the opportunity to develop their talents.

According to Nelson and Economy, (2005), employee development doesn't just happen. For employees to learn new skills and develop their expertise and knowledge, both managers and employees must make a concerted effort to ensure employment development stays at or near the top of everyone's list of priorities.

The Need for Employee Development

One primary purpose of a staff development program is to increase the knowledge and skills of employees and thereby increase the potential of the organization to attain its goals and objectives.

Staff development goals and objectives will continually change to meet the continually changing needs of individual staff members and the organization. One key reason for developing employees is that they will learn a variety of new skills that will make them better and more effective in their jobs. No only will they do a better job for their organizations, they will do a better job for their customers -- earning their long-term business and loyalty in the process.

According to Singh, 2005, the overarching goal of staff development should be to make employees productive citizens of the organization and of society. Approaching staff development from this broad perspective can pay rich dividends in better quality, improved morale, and higher commitment.

Another key reason for developing employees is to multiply the impact of your development efforts many times over. When you spend time developing your employees, you are sending a message loud and clear: Your employees are important to you and worth your time and attention. Employees who feel that you think they are important are employees who will become important, bringing with them a high level of loyalty and commitment.

Employee Development Process

Most training takes place on the job and in all probability this method is a most effective means of training and least costly to operate. Staff are placed in the actual work situation, which makes them feel immediately productive. They learn by doing.

Another approach to on-the-job training according to Rebore (1995) is job-instruction training, a more systematic approach to training developed during World War II which consists of preparing trainees by telling them about the job, presenting information essential to performing the job, having trainees demonstrates their understanding of the job, and placing trainees in the job on their own and assigning a resource person to assist the trainees if they need help.

There is off-the-job training as well referring to various kinds of programs such as workshops, case studies, programmed instruction and simulations. According to Rebore (1995), the business community in the last two decades has substantially increased the use of case studies, programmed instruction, and simulation exercises in training programs.

Whether it is on-the-job, off-the-job or apprenticeship training, the role of the manager in developing employees is to help them figure out exactly the areas where development will help to make them better and more productive workers in the future and provide them with the training, job orientation, support and organizational resources for employees to get there. Once needs are identified, plans developed, and resources identified, managers and employees can work together to turn them into reality.

Ask your staff about their careers. You need to determine the best way to the path your employees want to take in their careers and then you'll have a baseline from which to work. Discuss with your staff their strengths and weaknesses. Every employee has areas of weakness and strength. Assess where they are now (beginning, between, or end) in their career. By assessing the current state of their skills and talents, you'll end up with an overall road map to guide your development efforts. Create career development plans. This formalizes the agreements that you make to provide formal support or resources to your employees in developing their career. And finally, follow through on your agreements, and make sure that your staff follow through on theirs. Be sure to check your staff's progress regularly and if they miss schedules because of other priorities, reassign their work as necessary to ensure that they have the time they need to focus on their career development.

Mentoring, Coaching, and Counseling

Mentoring, coaching or counseling entails an informal discussion between the employee and the supervisor when an employee needs to make improvement. According to Singh 2005, counseling is a mild form of attention-getter that is devoid of any kind of threat to an individual's sense of job security.

Most business leaders are familiar with the power of mentoring, a relationship in which a person with greater experience and wisdom guides another to a higher level of personal and professional excellence. Mentors benefit organization by explaining how the organization really works. Employees learn by witnessing their mentors performing. It provides growth experiences and provides career guidance and discussion.

To be a mentor to an employee the manager needs to provide opportunities to learn and grow. Let the employee fill in for you in staff meetings. Assign your staff to a team. Allow them to pursue and develop their ideas. Provide them with a choice of assignments. Send them to a seminar on a new topic. Take an employee with you when you call on customers. Introduce your staff to top managers in your organization, and arrange to have him or her perform special assignments for them. The ultimate goal of mentoring, coaching and counseling is for the supervisors to help their staff attain better level of performance and behavioral change. More importantly, for staff to manage and be responsible for their own decision making.

CHAPTER TWELVE

STAFF PERFORMANCE APPRAISAL

"A task without a vision is drudgery; a vision without a task is a dream; a task with a vision is victory."

--Anonymous

"Whatever task you undertake, do it with all your heart and soul.
Always be courteous, never be discouraged. Beware of him who promises something for nothing. Do not blame anybody for your mistakes and failures. Do not look for approval except the consciousness of doing your best."

--Bernard M. Baruch

Instead of being a judgmental and punitive tool, the performance appraisal process should focus on staff development. Achieving this objective requires the participation of both the employee and the supervisor who does the evaluation. If the supervisors and the employees understand the organization's philosophy of staff development and its relationship to performance evaluation, the process will not be as difficult for both parties as it often turns out to be.

Performance appraisal is a part of management by objectives (MBO) and it should be based on a joint agreement between supervisors and employees on what specific and measurable objectives will be accomplished over a given time, and at the end of that time, the supervisors evaluate individual employees according to whether they have accomplished these objectives. (Bounds and Woods 1998).

Beyond supporting and encouraging the efforts of employees, coaching play a critical part of the learning process for staff who are developing their skills, knowledge, and self-confidence. Employees will never learn to be self-sufficient when manager is always telling them what to do. In fact, they usually don't learn at all, making them more reliant on you going forward, rather than less reliant. As the old saying goes: Tell me … I forget. Show me … I remember. Involve me … I learn.

The performance appraisal process includes day-to-day supervisor-employee interactions (coaching, counseling, disciplining); written documentation (making notes about an employee's behavior, completing the performance appraisal form); the formal appraisal interview; and follow-up sessions that may involve coaching/ and/or discipline when needed.

When managers are asked what they like best about their jobs, invariably "doing performance appraisals" is near the top of their lists. Among the reasons these managers give for disliking performance reviews are "You can't evaluate staff performance," "The form we use is lousy," "Our staff are professionals -- they don't need to be evaluated," "If you give someone a low rating, my boss won't back me up." Partly because such reasons, we find that people who do appraisals generally spend little time on them and tend to give everyone high ratings.

But what about their staff perspective on performance appraisal? Think back to your own most recent performance review and reflect on three questions: How prepared was the person who did the appraisal? How accurate was the feedback you received? Did the performance feedback session help you improve your performance? If your answers are "not very prepared," "not very accurate," and "didn't help me improve," then your comments are typical.

None of this, however, should be construed as a recommendation to do away with performance appraisals. Instead, this chapter is intended to provide information that will help managers do a better job of appraising their employees. Before getting into the specific "nuts and bolts" of doing appraisals, we must first understand the numerous factors that affect the way appraisals are done and the assumptions that underlie this chapter.

Staff Skills and Performance Problems

According Sullivan et al. (1992), some employees, even though highly motivated, simply do not have the abilities or skills to perform well. Abilities and skills play a major role in individual behavior and performance. Effective managers are proficient in matching each person's abilities and skills with the job requirement. The matching process is important since no amount of leadership, motivation, or organizational resources can make up for deficiencies in abilities or skills. Job analysis is a widely used technique that takes some of the guesswork out of matching. Job analysis is the process of defining and studying a job in terms of tasks or behaviors and specifying the responsibilities, education, and training needed to perform the job successfully (Ivancevich & Glueck, 1986).

Strategies that focus on congruence between ability and job requirements include recruitment efforts directed toward graduates of programs with sound professional curricula, selection methods that identify specific abilities/skills and match them with known employee characteristics, staff development programs that upgrade knowledge and skills of employees as job requirements change, and special programs such as intensive workshops and continuing education. The manager plays a crucial role in ongoing assessment and evaluation of employees, providing opportunities and encouragement for their advancement and maintenance of abilities. In addition, the manager is in the best position to communicate educational needs to the administration so that adequate resources are allocated for this function.

A desired result of any employee's behavior is effective job performance. An important part of the supervisor's job is to define performance in advance -- to state desired results. In organizations, individual and environmental variables affect not only behavior but also performance. Performance-related behaviors are directly associated with job tasks and need to be accomplished to achieve a job's objectives. From a supervisor's perspective, searching for ways to enhance performance includes such actions as identifying performance problems; planning, organizing, and controlling the work of employees; and creating a motivational climate for subordinates. If employees are not performing well or consistently, managers must investigate the problem. (Sullivan et al., 1992).

Job satisfaction has been divided into a number of components: interpersonal relations, achievement, responsibility, advancement, the work itself, recognition, supervision, working conditions, salary, and status. All of these relate in some way to employee productivity. Since managers focus their attention on performance-related behaviors, they search for ways to achieve optimal performance. If employees are not performing well or are performing inconsistently, managers must investigate the problems.

The first step in using this model is to begin with accepted standards of performance and an accurate assessment of the current performance of the staff member.

This means job descriptions must be current and performance appraisal tools must be written in behavioral terms. It also implies that employee evaluations are regularly carried out and implemented according to recognized guidelines.

Second, the manager must decide whether the problem demands immediate attention and whether it is a skill-related or motivation-related problem. Once these determinations are made, the manager can proceed to an appropriate plan of action. Skill-related problems can be solved through informal training, such as demonstration and coaching, whereas complex skills require formal training in the form of in-service sessions or workshops. If there are limitations regarding the length of time for an employee to reach the desired level of skill, the manager must determine whether the job could be simplified or whether the better decision would be to terminate or transfer the employee. In any deliberations, the manager must include budgetary considerations in the decision-making process. For example, would it be more cost-effective to hire an expert or experienced staff at a higher salary rather than to provide the necessary staff development to have the current employee reach a satisfactory performance level? Often, the resources of the organization determine which option the manager is able to exercise.

If the performance problem is motivation rather than ability, the manager must address a different set of questions. Specifically, whether the employee believes the behavior leads to punishment, reward, or inaction must be determined. If the "reward" for conscientiously coming to work on holidays (rather than calling in sick) leads to always being scheduled for holiday work, then good performance is associated with punishment. Only when the employee sees a strong link between valued outcomes and meeting performance expectations will motivation strategies succeed. The manager plays a role in tailoring motivational efforts to meet the individual needs of the employee. Unfortunately, creating a performance-reward climate does not eliminate all problem behaviors. When the use of rewards proves ineffective, other strategies, such as coaching and discipline, are warranted.

In attempting to differentiate between lack of ability and lack of motivation, an analysis of past performance is useful. If past performance has been acceptable and there has been little change in standards of performance, it is likely that the problem results from a lack of motivation. In contrast, if the staff has never performed at an acceptable level, the problem may be primarily skill related. Different intervention strategies should be used depending on whether the problem results from a lack of motivation or a lack of skill. The objective should be to enhance performance rather than to punish the employee.

Supervisors may be reluctant to effectively manage problem employees because of claims of discrimination or the feelings of anger and resentment that follow. To ensure that employee civil rights are respected, the manager should work closely with top administration and the human resources department. All employees deserve fair and equitable treatment; however, different responses by employees can lead to claims of discriminatory treatment. It is necessary to document problem behavior and adhere to the guidelines established by valid performance appraisals.

The credibility of the manager influences how well he or she is able to enhance employee performance. How the manager is viewed by employees in the leadership role determines the impact on the performance behavior of employees. If the manager is viewed as fair and genuinely interested in the welfare of each employee as an individual, he or she will facilitate employee motivation. Often the manager must walk a tight rope between empathy and objectivity in guiding employees to reach their potential.

The Needs and Importance of Performance Appraisals

Performance appraisals often are the basis upon which administrative decisions such as the size of a salary increase or who gets promoted are made (Murphy & Cleveland, 1991). Ideally, accurate appraisal information allows an organization to tie rewards to performance. Performance appraisals are also used for employee development. After a thorough review of an employee's performance, the supervisor and employee may jointly develop action plans to help the individual improve. Such developmental activities may include formal training, academic course work, or simple on-the-job coaching.

A final reason for doing performance reviews concerns fair employment practice law (e.g., Title VII of the 1964 Civil rights Act, Age Discrimination in Employment Act). Performance appraisals and the decisions, such as layoffs, based on those appraisals are covered by several federal and state laws. In the last two decades, numerous employees have successfully sued their organizations over employment decisions that were based on questionable performance appraisal results.

Regardless of how an organization uses performance appraisals, it is essential that they accurately reflect the employee's actual job performance. If performance ratings are inaccurate, an inferior employee may be promoted, another employee may not receive needed training, or there may not be a tie between performance and rewards (thus lessening employee motivation). All employees in the organization must understand clearly what is expected from them individually, commensurate with their qualifications and level of expertise. Figure 12:1 further illustrates this fact.

1. The appraisal should be in writing and carried out at least once a year.

2. The performance appraisal information should be shared with the employee.

3. The employee should have the opportunity to respond in writing to his or her appraisal.

4. Employees should have a mechanism to appeal the results of the performance appraisal.

5. The supervisor should have adequate opportunity to observe the employee's job performance during the course of the evaluation period. If adequate contact is lacking (e.g., the appraiser and the appraisee work different shifts), then appraisal information should be gathered from other sources.

6. Notes (critical incidents) on the employee's performance should be kept during the entire evaluation period. These notes should be shared with the employee during the course of the evaluation period.

7. Evaluators should be trained to carry out the performance appraisal process (e.g., what is reasonable job performance, how to complete the form, how to carry out the feedback interview).

8. Insofar as possible, the performance appraisal should focus on employee behavior and results rather than on personal traits or characteristics (e.g., initiative, attitude, personality).

Adapted from Sullivan Eleanor, J., Effective Management Nursing, 3rd Edition, © 1992, pp. 350-351. Reprinted by permission of Pearson Education, Inc., Upper Saddle River, NJ.

Figure 12:1   Non-Discriminatory Appraisal System

Reprimanding Employees

Before reprimanding an employee, it is wise to first give mentoring and counseling as stated earlier. Most managers dread having to reprimand an employee. Nevertheless, there will be occasions where discipline is necessary (e.g., when a regulation has been violated, thereby jeopardizing products or services). In viewing the discipline process, the manager must never lose sight of the reason for discipline. The primary function of discipline is not to punish the guilty party but to encourage that person and others to behave appropriately in the future. (Boncarosky, 1979).

When faced with a disciplinary situation, the manager should maintain close contact with the institution's human resource department and administration. Before taking any disciplinary action, the manager should discuss the action he or she intends to take and seek approval for it. This close coordination between the manager and the administration is essential to guarantee that any disciplinary action is administered in a fair and legally defensible manner.

To further ensure fairness, rules and regulations must be clearly communicated; a system of progressive penalties must be developed; and an appeals process must be available. To enforce rules or regulations, employees need to be informed of them ahead of time, preferably in writing.

An institution's staff development efforts can be regarded as successful when most of its staff Members employ self-discipline by adhering to rules and standards of acceptable behavior. But a few employees will not take on the responsibility of self-discipline. Such employees will require some form of extrinsic disciplinary action as outlined in Figure 12:2.

1. Getting the facts before acting. Make sure you are not disciplining or accusing falsely.

2. Do not act while angry. Control your temperament as you discipline.

3. Do not suddenly tighten your enforcement of rules. Give verbal and written warnings per policy.

4. Do not apply penalties inconsistently. Be fare at all times to everybody.

5. Discipline in private. The privacy gives the staff some integrity and the spirit is not broken.

6. Make the offense clear. Specify what is appropriate behavior.

7. Get the other side of the story. Always be attentive to what the staff has to say.

8. Do not let the disciplinary become personal. Discipline the behavior and not personality.

9. Do not back down when you are right. Maintain your correct point of view at all times.

10. Stay in touch with personnel. Always follow the organization's policy and procedure.

Adapted from Sullivan, Eleanor J., Effective Management Nursing, 3rd Edition © 1992, p. 369
Reprinted by permission of Pearson Education, Inc. Upper Saddle River, NJ.

Figure 12:2   Guidelines For Effective Discipline

Once disciplinary action has been deemed necessary, the approach to disciplining should be positive and progressive. A positive approach requires emphasis on the corrective, rather than punitive, nature of disciplinary action. If punishment is involved, it should be with the objective of correcting behavior otherwise, it may lead to adversarial relationships between employees and their supervisors. Although the supervisor and the employee engage in joint discussion and problem solving, nothing is imposed by management; all solutions and affirmations are jointly reached. Sherman et al. (1998) suggested that in positive disciplining, the total responsibility for correcting a problem is placed on the employee.

PART IV
LEADERSHIP AND SERVING

"Self-reverence, self-knowledge, self-control, these three alone lead life to sovereign power"

--Alfred Lord Tennyson

CHAPTER THIRTEEN

SERVING LEADERSHIP

"Whatever authority I may have rests solely on knowing how little I know"

--Socrates

In his book Servant Leadership, Robert Greenleaf ,(2002), asserted that the servant-leader begins with the natural feeling that one wants to serve first. Servant-leader conscious choice to serve first brings one to aspire to lead. This choice is different from one who is leader first - a later choice to serve after leadership is established, because of the need to assuage an unusual power drive or to acquire material possessions. According to Greenfield, "the difference manifests itself in the care taken by the servant-first to make sure that other people's highest priority needs are being served."

Power-leader has the ability to control the behavior of others. A person has power when she or he is able to make other people do what he or she wants them to. Argenti (1994) says this is the ability to motivate someone to do something that they would otherwise not do. The President or Chief Executive Officer of any organization has the power to order employees to act to implement the goals of the facility as expressed in the policies and plans.

Webster's New World Dictionary (2006) gives 14 definitions for the word power. An additional half-dozen synonyms indicate that power denotes the inherent ability or the admitted right to rule, govern, determine, control, regulate, restrain, and curb. Power is a complex concept in our modern age and serving-leaders seldom use it to the extreme.

Guidelines for Serving Leadership

Bennis, et al, (2001, p. 111), assert that "since the world is moving too fast for the cumbersome rigidities of authoritarian control, and since a leader's most important tool is the leader's own personality, all potential leaders need to ask is leadership questions of their ego."

Effective leaders should be willing to make decisions, but should also allow members of their group to work as they see fit. (Bennis and Biederman, 1997, p. 20).

"Leadership should not be so much the exercise of power itself as the empowerment of others, and the idea that the leader controls, directs, prods, manipulates is perhaps the most damaging myth of all." (Bennis and Nanus, 1985, pp. 224-225).

"The leader must be willing and be able to set up reliable mechanisms of feedback so that he can not only conceptualize the social territory of which he is an important part, but realize how he influences it" (Bennis and Slater, 1999, p. 127).

Christian Leadership

An effective Christian leadership is illustrated in 1 Timothy 3:1-7, NIV. "Here is a trustworthy saying: If anyone sets his heart on being an overseer, he desires a noble task. Now the overseer must be above reproach, the husband of but one wife, temperate, self-controlled, respectable, hospitable, able to teach, not given to much wine, not violent but gentle, not quarrelsome, not a lover of money. He must manage his own family well and see that his children obey him with proper respect. (If anyone does not know how to manage his own family, how can he take care of God's church?) He must not be a recent convert, or he may become conceited and fall under the same judgment as the devil. He must also have a good reputation with outsiders, so that he will not fall into disgrace and into the devil's trap."

In Galatians 5:22,23, Paul clearly states that Christ desires that His followers manifest some distinct characters. The character-building fruits to become identical with the characters of Jesus: "But the fruit of the Spirit is love, joy, peace, longsuffering, goodness, faith, meekness, temperance: against such there is no law." All these fruits have to be cultivated to be an effective Christian leader.

Christ Himself instructs us on leadership by demonstrating greatness in serving when He said in John 13:12-17 "So when He had washed their feet, taken His garments, and sat down again, He said to them, "Do you know what I have done to you? You call Me Teacher and Lord, and you say well, for so I am. If I then, your Lord and Teacher, have washed your feet, you also ought to wash one another's feet. For I have given you an example, that you should do as I have done to you. Most assuredly, I say to you, a servant is not greater than his master; nor is he who is sent greater than he who sent him. If you know these things, blessed are you if you do them."

When the disciples argue about greatness Christ answered them in Matthew 20:25-27; Mark 10:42-44 and Luke 22:25-27 saying "The kings of the Gentiles exercise lordship over them, and those who exercise authority over them are called benefactors. But not so among you; on the contrary, he who is greatest among you, let him be as the younger, and he who governs as he who serves. For who is greater, he who sits at the table, or he who serves? Is it not he who sits at the table? Yet I am among you as the One who serves."

Paul writing to the Romans on serving with spiritual gifts says in Romans 12:3

"For I say, through the grace giving to me, to everyone who is among you, not to think of himself more highly than he ought to think, but to think soberly, as God has dealt to each one a measure of faith."

Concepts presented by Ellen G. White on leadership are supported by contemporary authors and researchers alike. Her written materials appear to warn against authoritarian leadership and strongly support democratic leadership.

"To no man," she said, "has been appointed the work of being a ruler over his fellow men. Every man is to bear his own burden." (White, MS, 1907). She recommended the study of the first two chapters of Ezekiel. The wheels within a wheel, she said, represents confusion to the finite eye. But a hand of infinite wisdom was revealed amid the wheels. Perfect order was brought out of confusion. (White, MS, 1907).

Here was democracy in action. "in our several callings there is to be mutual dependence on one another for assistance" (White, LT, 1903). Again under the heading, "A Council of Men-Not Just One Man," she said, "The power vested in the conference is not to be centered in one man, or two men, or six men; there is to be a council of men over the separate divisions." (White, MS, 1907).

"Take unto you the whole armor of God, and never forget the gospel shoes of peace. Go not to any man with a heavy treat or with anger in your voice. Let all God's servants, from those occupying the highest positions, to those in the lowliest service, walk humbly before Him. (White, Manuscript 140, 1902).

Authoritarian management must change, she said. In addition, she admonished that no one control human minds. The presidents of conferences are being imbued with a spirit to rule, to require men to bow to their judgment; if they refuse, the course persuaded toward them is such as to fill heaven with indignation. Our institutions need cleansing as did the temple when Christ was upon the earth. Man lords it over men's consciences, man dictates to his fellowmen as God. Everywhere this spirit is leaving hearts with the same narrow and selfish purposes. Reaction must come and who shall then set things in order? Jesus says, 'He that will come after me, let him deny himself, and take up his cross daily and follow me.' (White, LT, 1903).

It seems clear that God's work has no room for authoritarianism. The man who, because he is president of a conference (and, perhaps, institutions are included) dares to take the responsibility of telling his fellow workers what their duty is, is working out a wrong experience. The influence will be to destroy   the God-given personality of men, and place them under human jurisdiction. Such management is laying a foundation for unbelief. (White, LT, 1907).

Leadership is not Lordship -- But it is the devising of men that leads to oppression, injustice and wickedness. The cause of God is to be free from every taint of injustice. It can gain no advantage by robbing the members of the family of God of their individuality or their rights. All such practices are abhorrent to God. The high-handed power that has been developed, as though positions had made men gods, makes me afraid, and ought to cause fear. It is a curse whenever, and by whomsoever, it is exercised. This lording it over God's heritage will create such a disgust of man's jurisdiction that a state of insubordination will result. (White, LT, 1907).

Dictators should be replaced by leaders filled with the Holy Spirit-leaders who know democratic management techniques in leading God's church during this crucial time in history. Ellen White stated: If a man is sanguine of his own powers and seeks to exercise dominion over his brethren, feeling that he is invested with authority to make his will the ruling power, the best and only safe course is to remove him, lest great harm be done, and he lose his own soul, and imperil the souls of others.... A man's position does not make him one jot or title greater in the sight of God; it is character alone that God values. (White, LT, 1907).

Let no man be placed in a position where he can lord it over God's heritage; for this imperils alike the soul of him who rules and the souls of those who are under his rule." (White, LT, 1907). In writing about management of sanitariums, Ellen White said, "No man is ever to set himself up as a ruler, as a lord over his fellowmen.... No one man's voice and influence should ever be allowed to become a controlling power. (White, *Medical Ministry*, 1932, pp. 164, 165).

Praying Leadership -- Every Christian leader needs prayer. Christ Himself prayed and gave instructions to pray in season and without season in Matthew 17:21; 21:22 and Mk. 9:29. There is help for the leader who feels inadequate. James 1:5, NIV. Says "If any one of you lacks wisdom, he should ask God who gives generously to all without finding fault, and it will be given to him."

Ellen G. White says "the path of men who are placed as leaders is not an easy one. But they are to see in every difficulty a call to prayer. Never are they to fail of consulting the great Source of all wisdom. Strengthened and enlightened by the Master Worker, they will be enabled to stand firm against unholy influences and to discern right from wrong, good from evil. They will approve that which God approves, and will strive earnestly against the introduction of wrong principles into His cause. (White, Prophets and Kings, pp. 30-31; Testimonies, Vol. 5, p. 423; Testimonies to Ministers, pp. 323-4).

Kindness, Courtesy, and the Lowliness of Christ -- Paul in Philippians 2:3-4 talking about unity through humility states "Let nothing be done through selfish ambition or conceit, but in lowliness of mind let each esteem others better than himself. Let each of you look out not only for his own interests, but also for the interests of others."

Paul in 2 Timothy 2:24,25 continues saying that "a servant of the Lord must not quarrel but be gentle to all, able to teach, patient, in humility correcting those who are in opposition, if God perhaps will grant them repentance, so that they may know the truth." He continues in Titus 3:2 saying "to speak evil of no one, to be peaceable, gentle, showing all humility to all men."

Ellen G. White says "you need the kindness, courtesy, meekness, and lowliness of Christ. You may have valuable qualifications that can be perfected for highest service if sanctified to God. You should feel the necessity of approaching your brethren with kindness and courtesy, not with harshness and severity. You do not realize the harm you do by your sharp, domineering spirit toward them." (White, Letter 3, 1888, p. Jan. 10, 1888).

"We may never know until the judgment the influence of a kind, considerate course of action to the inconsistent, the unreasonable, and unworthy. If after a course of provocation and injustice on their part, you treat them as you would an innocent person, you even take pains to show them special acts of kindness, then you have acted the part of a Christian, and they become surprised and ashamed and see their course of action and meanness more clearly than if you plainly stated their aggravated acts to rebuke them." (White, Letter 20, 1892 October 17, 1892 to J.H. Kellogg).

God Exalts the Humble -- Christ Jesus talking about who is the greatest gave to His disciples says in Matthew 18:4 that "whoever humbles himself as this little child is the greatest in the kingdom of heaven. Luke 22:25, NIV. "Jesus said to them, 'The kings of the Gentiles lord it over them; and those who exercise authority over them call themselves Benefactors. But you are not to be like that. Instead, the greatest among you should be like the youngest, and the one who rules like the one who serves.'" Ellen G. White wrote that "He is most fit to carry responsibilities and command who most resembles God in character, in goodness, mercy, and staunch loyalty to the cause and work of God. Every one needs now to work for brother, for friend, for neighbor, and for stranger, drawing the mind away from the discouragements that will crowd in. The truth is to be magnified. We must not be surprised at strange movements. No one must seek exaltation. The more humbly we move and work, the more will we be exalted with God. The return of Jesus Christ to our world will not be long delayed. This is to be the keynote of every message." (White, Letter 39, 1898, p. 13 March 27, 1898 to Brethren Woods and Miller).

Position Does Not Give Holiness -- Ellen White says "Solomon was never so rich or so wise or so truly great as when he confessed, 'I am but a little child: I know not how to go out or come in.' Those who today occupy positions of trust should seek to learn the lesson taught by Solomon's prayer. The higher the position a man occupies, the greater the responsibility that he has to bear, the wider will be the influence that he exerts and the greater his need of dependence on God. Ever should he remember that with the call to work comes the call to walk circumspectly before his fellow men. He is to stand before God in the attitude of a learner. Position does not give holiness of character. It is by honoring God and obeying His commands that a man is made truly great. So long as he remains consecrated, the man who God has endowed with discernment and ability will not manifest an eagerness for high position, neither will he seek to rule or control. Of necessity men must bear responsibilities; but instead of striving for the supremacy, he who is a true leader will pray for an understanding heart, to discern between good and evil." (White, Prophets and Kings, pp. 30-31).

Patience and Courage -- A good leader must exercise patience and courage.

Proverbs 16:32, NIV. Says, "Better a patient man than a warrior, a man who controls his temper than one who takes a city."

Anyone who has had courage -- "moral courage to call these things by their right name, and who has refused to be drawn into the net spread for the unwary, who would not be robbed without making a protest, were not looked upon with favor by those with whom they disagreed. Members of councils and boards who would not uphold exaction and double-dealing, but who took a firm stand for the right, were not invited to be present at the meetings where these plans were discussed." (White, Letter 4, 1896, pp. 13, 15, 16 (July 1, 1896 To Men in Responsible Positions).

Unbending Integrity -- Paul in the 2 Corinthians 7:2 on integrity says "receive us; we have wronged no man, we have corrupted no man, we have defrauded no man" Every leader should be able to repeat Psalms 25:21, NIV. "May integrity and uprightness protect me, because my hope is in you."

Ellen G. White says "an honest man, according to Christ's measurement, is one who will manifest unbending integrity. Deceitful weights and false balances, with which many seek to advance their interests in the world, are abomination in the sight of God. When a man is indeed connected with God, and is keeping His law in truth, his life will reveal the fact; for all his actions will be in harmony with the teachings of Christ. He will not sell his honor for gain. His principles are built upon the sure foundation, and his conduct in worldly matters is a transcript of his principles. Firm integrity shines forth as gold amid the dross and rubbish of the world. Deceit, falsehood, and unfaithfulness may be glossed over and hidden from the eyes of man, but not from the eyes of God." (White, Testimonies, Volume 4, p. 310-311).

Recognize Limitations and Credit Others With Some Sense -- Deuteronomy 1:9, NIV. "At that time I said to you, 'You are too heavy a burden for me to carry alone.'" "Leading men should place responsibilities upon others, and allow them to plan and devise and execute, so that they may obtain an experience. Give them a word of counsel when necessary, but do not take away the work because you think the brethren are making mistakes. May God pity the cause when one man's mind and one man's plan are followed without question. God would not be honored should such a state of things exist. All workers must have room to exercise their own judgment and discretion. God has given men and women talents which He means that they should use. He has given them minds and He means that they should become thinkers, and do their own thinking and planning rather than depend upon others to think and plan for them." (White, Letter 12, 1885, October 28, 1885, To Butler and Haskell).

Teamwork -- Effective leaders delegate, supervise, affirm and show appreciation for the work of others. Exodus 39:43, NIV. "Moses inspected the work and saw that they had done it just as the Lord had commanded. So Moses blessed them." A good leader seeks counsel from others. Proverbs 15:22, NIV. "Plans fail for lack of counsel, but with many advisers they succeed."

"By means of one agency, Christ Jesus, God has mysteriously linked all men together. To every man He has assigned some special line of service; and we should be quick to comprehend that we are to guard against leaving the work given us in order that we may interfere with other human agencies who are doing a work not precisely the same as our own. To no man has been assigned the work of interfering with the work of one of his fellow-laborers, trying to take it in hand himself; for he would so handle it that he would spoil it. To one, God gives a work different from the work that He gives another." (White Manuscript 29, 1907, pp. 9, 10. Individual Responsibility and Christian Unity, Jan. 1907; Letter 49, Sept. 1897, Workers in our Institutions; Testimonies, Volume 7, p. 259).

Serving and Influencing

Christian leaders are to demonstrate the acts and spirit of serving leadership. In their book *Managing By Values*, (1997), Ken Blanchard and Michael O'Connor illustrate leadership with *"SERVE"* as the five ways to reach full potential. "Is he a serving leader or a self serving leader?"

Seeing the future or visioning the future of the group. State your goals and your strategies. Leader's values should be stated, published, repeated, recognized, and rewarded with positive results.

Engaging and developing others. Peter Drucker said the most important decision an executive makes is "who does what". Fit people, and do not fix them in the right jobs. Make your goals clear. Train them well. Give them the right information. Have confidence in your subordinates. Be there when they need you. Let them know they are making a contribution and that leader and staff are both learning and growing. By developing subordinates, recruit and select the right people for the right job and engaging their hearts, heads, brain and hands.

Reinventing continuously. "The very best leaders are learners" -- reading, viewing, listening or spending time with mentors. Reinvent on personal level and on the organization how to work better, faster, with fewer errors and doing it for less.

Valuing results and relationships by listening, inventing time, caring deeply and accentuating the positive. To maximize results is to have high expectations for both results and relationships. The old saying "people will not care how much you know until they know how much you care."

Embody or live the value. For the subordinates to reach their full potential, the leader must gain their trust. The leader must live the values of the organization in order for him or her to be successful. "You must walk the talk." "Say it and show it."

According to Ken Blanchard and Michael O'Connor (1997), Christian leaders are challenged to continue emulating the skills, styles, and character that spells *"INFLUENCE."* Integrity -- building relationship on trust. Nurturing -- caring about people as individuals. Faith -- believing and trusting in people. Listening -- valuing what others have to say. Understanding -- seeing from their point of view. Enlarging -- helping others become bigger. Navigating -- assisting others through difficulties. Connecting -- initiating positive relationships and Empowering -- giving subordinates the power to lead.

Christ is the greatest leadership role model of all. He cares about people and results. He lived the values. His organization has been around for two thousand years. How many Fortune 100 Companies will be around in two hundred years let alone two thousand years from now? Christ selected twelve inexperienced people and developed them into leaders who could carry on after he was no longer there in bodily form. He showed a servant heart of leading by following. He showed to be the first by being the last. He came to serve at the last supper. He talked about the future. He engaged his followers. He challenged others to change self, to change others and to change the organization.

An effective Christian leader or servant-leader will be an example of hard work as it is stated in Ecclesiastes 9:10, NIV. "Whatever your hand finds to do, do it with all your might, for in the grave, where you are going, there is neither working nor planning nor knowledge nor wisdom." The leader will treat those under his or her leadership like he or she would like to be treated. Luke 6"31, NIV. says "Do to others as you would have them do to you."

Effective leaders plan ahead. The leader needs to have a sense for the unknowable and be able to foresee the unforeseeable. Leaders should know some things and foresee some things that those they are presuming to lead do not know or foresee as clearly. This is partly what gives them their "lead," what puts them out ahead and qualifies them to show the way. Luke 14:28-30, NIV says "Suppose one of you wants to build a tower. Will he not first sit down and estimate the cost to see if he has enough money to complete it? For if he lays the foundation and is not able to finish it, everyone who sees it will ridicule him, saying, 'This fellow began to build and was not able to finish.'"

The principles of management we find illustrated in the Bible includes sharing the work load. Exodus 18:21, NIV. Says "But select capable men from all the people - men who fear God, trustworthy men who hate dishonesty gain - and appoint them as officials over thousands, hundreds, fifties and tens."

CHAPTER FOURTEEN

EPILOGUE: AN OVERVIEW OF INEFFECTIVE AND EFFECTIVE LEADERSHIP

"Ability will enable a man to get to the top, but it takes character to keep him there. Moreover, you can always tell luck from ability by its duration"

-- Author Unknown

Dr. Henry Cloud in his book, *Integrity*, (2006), asserted that people who become leaders are at least expected to have three qualities. *Competencies* such as knowing their field, their industry and their discipline. There are a lot of people who are competent and good at what they do, are happy and fulfilled but do not get to be leaders or successful.

For someone to get to the level of a successful accomplishment, he or she must possess the second quality known as *forming or building an alliance or networking* with others who have competencies and resources and form relationships that are mutually beneficial. These leaders create alliances by forging relationships and partnerships with other people like investors, regulators, distribution channels, their boards and city government.

There are many examples of ethical lapses from the top business and government, all the way to the church that caused some major losses of individual careers, entire company collapse and government failure. If a CEO is truly going to successfully lead, according to Cloud, he or she has to have the third quality of *character with integrity*.

If leaders have good character, their ethics and integrity will be such that they can be trusted and they will not be duplicitous. Trusting a leader is a character that is bedrock, foundational, and without which we have nothing.

Dr. Henry Cloud went to say that character, integrity, morals and ethics under gird our entire system of business, relationships, government, finance, education, and our very lives. By way of our honesty, trustworthiness, faithfulness, dependability, honorability and the ability to do the right thing when no one is watching.

Ineffective Leadership Overview

This chapter concludes my view on effective leadership management. I quite agree that there are many different kinds of ineffective leaders, all of whom are frustrating to follow. Though this book does not talk particularly about ineffective leadership but they do exist out there. In her book *Bad Leadership*, Barbara Kellerman, (2004) asserted that after she has looked at hundreds of contemporary cases involving bad leaders and bad followers in the private, public, and nonprofit sectors, and in domains both domestic and international, she found that ineffective or bad leadership falls into several groups. Here are a few particularly difficult examples:

1. Incompetent leadership -- is when the leader lacks the will or skill (or both) to sustain effective action and does not create positive change. Incompetent leaders are ineffective, and they often stay that way. Poet and critic Samuel Johnson said, "Advice is seldom welcome, and those who need it most like it the least."

Incompetent leaders are not necessarily incompetent in every aspect. Some leaders lack practical, academic, or emotional intelligence (Goleman, 2002, pp. 301-321). Others are careless, dense, distracted, slothful, or sloppy, or they are easily undone by uncertainty and stress, unable effectively to communicate, educate, or delegate. It is important to note that the impact of incompetent leadership is highly variable. Sometimes, as in the case of pilot error, it leads to disaster. At other times it amounts to mere bungling.

Incompetent leaders are trouble, not only for the people they lead, but also for their entire organization. As John Maxwell once said, "they are "lids" on the parts of the organization they lead. The Law of the

Lid states in *The 21 Irrefutable Laws of Leadership*, "Leadership ability determines a person's level of effectiveness.""

2. Rigid Leadership -- *is when* the leader is stiff and unyielding. Although he may be competent, he is unable or unwilling to adapt to new ideas, new information, or changing times.

Rigid leader can be described by Barbara Tuchman's phrase "wooden-headed" -- a leader who consistently refuses to be "defeated by the facts. (Tuchman, 1984, p. 7). Rigid leaders can be successful up to a point. But if they refuse to change with the changing world, the result will be bad leadership.

3. Intemperate Leadership -- is when the leader lacks self-control.

In their book *Leadership on the Line*, Ronald Heifetz and Marty Linsky cautioned leaders to control their impulses: "We all have hungers that are expressions of our normal human needs. But sometimes those hungers disrupt our capacity to act wisely or purposefully." (Heifetz, & Linsky, 2002, p. 164). Because we live in a time when all top leaders are grist for media mill, the risk of such disruption is far greater than it was in the past.

4. Callous Leadership -- is when the leader is uncaring or unkind.

5. Corrupt or Selfish Leadership -- is when the leader lie, cheat, steal, and put self-interest ahead of the public interest to a degree that exceeds the norm.

The selfish leader will attempt to lead others for their own gain and for the detriment of others. These leaders believe that life is a point driven, zero-sum game, with winners and losers. They encourage others to be losers in the game of life so they can collect all the spoils for themselves.

A selfish leader advances at the expense of everyone around him or her. He or she should not selfishly hoard all the perks that come with his leadership position. Share whatever you have with the people below you. Legendary basketball coach John Wooden said that to be successful "you must be interested in finding the best way, not in having your own way".

Corrupt leaders are usually motivated by power or greed -- by the desire, in any case, to acquire more of a scarce resource. For example, to make more money, corrupt leaders take bribes, sell favors, evade taxes, exaggerate corporate earnings, engage in insider trading, cook the books, defraud governments and businesses, and in other ways cut corners, bend rules, and break the law.

6. Insular leadership -- is when the leader minimizes or disregards the health and welfare of the other - such as, those outside of the group or organization for which they are directly responsible.

hacked to death, even in a distant land.

7. Evil Leadership -- is when the leader commit atrocities. He or she use pain as an instrument of power. The harm done to men, women, and children is severe rather than slight. The harm can be physical, psychological, or both.

Evil leaders are not necessarily sadistic. But some experts argue that our notion of evil should include the intent not only to terrorize but also to prolong suffering. They believe that all evildoers derive some sort of satisfaction from hurting others (Psychiatrist Michael Weiner, 2002, p. 32).

8. Insecure or Controlling Leadership -- is when the leader think everything is about him, and as a result, every action, every piece of information , every decision is put through his filter of self-centeredness. When someone on their team performs exceptionally well, they fear being outshone, and they often try to keep him from rising up. When someone on their team does poorly, they react in anger because it makes them look bad.

Insecure leader desire the status quo -- for everyone but himself. In an organization, security flows downward. When a leader is insecure, he will often project that insecurity down to the people below him. John Maxwell said that "if you work for an insecure person, not only will you have to work to deflect that individual's insecurity from yourself, but you will also have to work hard to break the chain and create security for the people who work for you."

It is difficult to generate momentum when the person you work for is continually interrupting your progress by micromanaging you. Leader who micromanage others are often driven by one of two things: the desire for perfection, which is unobtainable, or the belief that no one can do a job as well as they can, which really boils down to their thinking others' contributions aren't as valuable as their own.

9. Visionless Leadership -- is when leader stopped forecasting or thinking about the present and the future of the organization. Leader who lack vision create two immediate problems for the people who work for them. First, they fail to provide direction or incentive to move forward. The ancient Proverbs author wrote, "Where there is no vision, the people perish." Second, leadership who lacks vision almost always lack passion. He or she have no fire -- and no fuel to keep the organization going.

10. Chameleon or Political Leadership -- leader who flip-flop and cannot be pinned down. When people follow a chameleon leader, they never know how he will react.

Political leader can be as difficult to pin down as well, but where emotional issues often fuel the chameleon leader's problems, political leaders are motivated by the desire to get ahead. It's hard to follow leader whose decisions are based on problematical ambitions rather than the mission or the good of the organization. He or she like the mayor who was asked where he stood on a particular issue. He answered, "Well, some of my friends are for it. Some are against it. As for me, I'm for my friends."

The world had enough ineffective leaders. What we need are good and effective leadership and I hope the readers of this book will agree with the fact that there is no easy formula for being a leader.   Leadership is challenging -- all those balancing acts, all the responsibility, all that pressure. And yet, good leadership happens -- and it comes in all kinds of packages. There are quite leaders and bombastic ones. There are analytical leaders and more impulsive ones. Some are tough as nails with their teams, others more nurturing. On the surface, you would be hard-pressed to say what qualities these leaders share.

Underneath, you would surely see that they best care passionately about their people -- about their growth and success. And you would see that they themselves are comfortable in their own skin. They are real, filled with candor, honesty, integrity, optimism and humanity.

Many people ask if leaders are born or made. The answer, of course, is both. Some characteristics, like IQ and energy, seem to come with the package. On the other hand, you learn some leadership skills, like self-confidence, at home and at school, in academics and sports. You learn others at work through iterative experience -- trying something, getting it wrong and learning from it, or getting it right and gaining the self-confidence to do it again, only better.

Leaders can have and should have good effect on their subordinates by following certain principles and guidelines outlined in this book.

Effective Leadership Overview

It is difficult to pick an issue of Fortune Magazine or the Wall Street Journal and not see a story of a leader who has derailed. Stories of executives such as Douglas Ivester of Coca Cola or Durk Jager of Procter & Gamble who are fired after disastrous starts as CEO. Unfortunately, it is all too rare to profile a CEO like Jack Welch, who has stayed at the top of his game for close to two decades. Effective leaders focus on what energizes. They are resilient, and they reinvent themselves. (Bennis et al, 2001).

As we become a nation of large and small institutions - churches, businesses, governments, labor unions, universities - it is important to pay more attention to their leadership qualities and characteristics. Big institutions are not serving us well and it will not make any sense to stand outside and criticize. Nothing of substance will happen unless there are people inside these institutions who are able to (and want to) lead them into better performance for efficiency, effectiveness and for the public good.

In his book, "Winning" Jack and Suzy Welch (2005), asserted leadership rules by describing principles and habits of effective leaders.

Life would be easier if leadership was just a list of simple rules, but paradoxes are inherent to the trade. That's part of fun of leading, though -- each day is a challenge. It is a brand-new chance to get better at a job that, when all is said and done, you can never be perfect at. You can only give everything you've got. Let's take a closer look at this idea of effective leadership management (ELM).

1. **Effective leadership management should relentlessly upgrade their team, using every encounter as an opportunity to evaluate, coach, and build self-confidence.**

After the Miami Heat finally broke a thirteen-year drought and won the NBA Championship, you couldn't turn on the TV or open a paper without hearing speculation as to why 2006 was "the year." There were theories about everything, from Dwayne Wade to Shaq O'Neill.

Most people agreed that the reason wasn't mysterious at all. The Miami Heat had the best players. The coaching staff was the season's best. And they were all bound together by a winning spirit so palpable you could feel it in the air.

There are lucky breaks and bad calls in any season, but the team with the best players usually does win. And that is why, very simply, you need to invest the vast majority of your time and energy as a leader in three activities.

* You have to evaluate -- making sure the right people are in the right jobs, supporting and advancing those who are, and moving out those who are not.

* You have to coach -- guiding, critiquing, and helping people to improve their performance in every way.

* And finally, you have to build self-confidence -- pouring out encouragement, caring, and recognition.

* Self-confidence energizes, and it gives your people the courage to stretch, take risks, and achieve beyond their dreams. It is the fuel of winning teams.

Too often, managers think that people development occurs once a year in performance reviews. That's not true. People development should be a daily event, integrated into every aspect of leadership regular goings-on.

Take budget reviews. They are a perfect occasion to focus on people. Leaders need to talk about the business and its results, but in a budget review he or she can really see team dynamics in action. If everyone around the table sits silent and frozen while the team leader pontificates, he or she has some serious coaching to do. If everyone's involved in the presentation and the whole team is alive, the manager has a great opportunity to give immediate feedback that the manager likes what he or she sees. If the team has a real star or a dud in its midst, it will be wise for the manager to share his or her impressions with its leader as soon as possible.

There should not be any event in manager's day that cannot be used for people development. Customer visits are a chance to evaluate sales force. Plant tours are an opportunity to meet promising new line managers and see if they have the ability to run something bigger. A tea break at a meeting is an opening to coach a team member who is about to give his first major presentation.

And remember in all these encounters, evaluating and coaching are great, but building self confidence is, in the end, probably the most important thing you can do. Take every opportunity to inject self-confidence into those who have earned it. Use ample praise, the more specific the better.

Besides its huge impact on upgrading the team, the best thing about using every encounter for people development is how much fun it is. Instead of mind-numbing meetings about numbers and plant tours showing off new machines, every day is about growing people. In fact, the manager should think of him or her self as a gardener, with a watering can in one hand and a can of fertilizer in the other. Occasionally he or she has to pull some weeds, but most of the time, just nurture and tend.

2. Effective leadership management should make sure people not only see the vision, they live and breathe it.

It goes without saying that leaders have to set the team's vision and most do. But there's so much more to the "vision thing" than that. Leader has to make the vision come alive.

How do you achieve that? First of all, no jargon. Goals cannot sound noble but vague. Targets cannot be so blurry they can't be hit. Leadership direction has to be so vivid that if one of your employees is randomly woken up in the middle of the night and asked him or her "Where are we going?" he or she could still answer in a half-asleep stupor, "We're going to keep improving our service to individual contractors and expand our market aggressively reaching out to small wholesalers."

One of the most common problems in organizations is that leaders communicate the vision to their closest colleagues and its implications never filter down to people in frontline positions. Think about all the times you have bumped into a rude or harried clerk at a high-service department store, or been put on hold by a call center operator at a company that promises speed and convenience.

Somehow, they haven't heard the mission, maybe because it wasn't shouted in their direction, loud enough or often enough. Or maybe their rewards weren't aligned.

And that's the final piece of this particular leadership habit. If you want people to live and breathe the vision, "show them the money" when they do, be it with salary, bonus, or significant recognition of some sort. A company's compensation plans determine how its people behave.

Vision is an essential element of the leader's job. But no vision is worth the paper it's printed on unless it is communicated constantly and reinforced with rewards. Only then will it leap off the page-and come to life.

3. Effective leadership management should get into everyone's skin, exuding positive energy and optimism.

The old saying "The fish rots from the head." It's mainly used to refer to how politics and corruption filter down into an organization, but it could just as easily be used to describe the effect of a bad attitude at the top of any team, large or small. Eventually, everyone's infected.

The leader's mood is, for lack of a better word, catching. You've seen the dynamic a hundred times. An upbeat manager who goes through the day with a positive outlook somehow ends up running a team or organization filled with upbeat people with positive outlooks.

Sometimes there are good reasons to be down. When the economy is bad, and when competition is brutal. Yes, life and work can be tough. But your job as leader is to fight the gravitational pull of negativism. That doesn't mean you sugarcoat the challenges your team faces. It does mean you display an energizing, can-do attitude about overcoming them. It means you get out of your office and into everyone's skin, really caring about what they're doing and how they're faring as you take the hill together.

I've seen a few capable managers run their businesses while keeping their people at arm's length. These managers often demonstrated the right values, like candor and rigor, and they delivered good results.

4. Effective leadership management should establish trust with candor, transparency, and credit.

For some people, becoming a leader can be a real power trip. They relish the feeling of control over both people and information. And so they keep secrets, reveal little of their thinking about people and their performance, and hoard what they know about the business and its future.

This kind of behavior certainly establishes the leader as boss, but it drains trust right out of a team. Trust happens when leaders are transparent, candid, and keep their word. It's that simple.

Your people should always know where they stand in terms of their performance. They have to know how the business is doing. And sometimes the news is not good --such as imminent layoffs -- and any normal person would rather avoid delivering it. But you have to fight the impulse to pad or diminish hard messages or you'll pay with your team's confidence and energy.

Leaders also establish trust by giving credit where credit is due. They never score off their own people by stealing an idea and claiming it as their own. They don't kiss up and kick down because they are self-confident and mature enough to know that their team's success will get them recognition, and sooner rather than later. In bad times, leaders take responsibility for what's gone wrong. In good times, they generously pass around the praise.

When you become a leader, sometimes you really feel the pull to say, "Look at what I've done." When your team excels, it's only normal to want some credit yourself.

After all, you run the show. You hand out the paychecks, so people listen to your every word (or pretend to) and they laugh at all your jokes (or pretend to). In some companies, being boss means getting a special parking place or traveling first class. It could go to your head. You could really start to feel pretty big.

Refuse to be classified as bad leadership (some traits will be mentioned later). Remember, when you were made a leader you weren't given a crown, you were given a responsibility to bring out the best in others. For that, your people need to trust you. And they will, as long as you demonstrate candor, give credit, and stay real.

5. Effective leadership management should have the courage to make unpopular decisions and gut calls.

By nature, some people are consensus builders. Some people long to be loved by everyone. Those behaviors can really get you in the soup if you are a leader, because no matter where you work or what you do, there are times you have to make hard decisions -- let people go, cut funding to a project, or close a plant.

Obviously, tough calls spawn complaints and resistance. Your job is to listen and explain yourself clearly but move forward.

You are not a leader to win a popular contest -- you are a leader to lead. Don't run for office. You're already elected.

Sometimes making a decision is hard not because it's unpopular, but because it comes from your gut and defies a "technical" rationale. Leaders are faced with gut calls all the time. You're asked to invest in a new office building, for instance, but visiting the city, you see cranes in every direction. The deal's numbers are absolutely perfect, you're told, but you've been here before. You know that overcapacity is around the corner and the "perfect" investment is about to be worth sixty cents on the dollar. You've got no proof, but you've got a real strange feeling in your stomach.

You have to kill the idea, even if that pisses people off. Sometimes the hardest gut calls involve picking people. You meet a candidate who has all the right stuff. His resume is perfect: prestigious schools and great experience. His interview is impressive: firm handshakes, good eye contact, smart questions, and so on. But something nags at you. Maybe he's moved around an awful lot -- he's just had too many jobs in too few years without a plausible enough explanation. Or his energy seems too frantic. Or one previous boss said nice things about him but didn't sound as though he really meant them.

6. Effective leadership management should probe and push with a curiosity that borders on skepticism, making sure their questions are answered with action.

When you are an individual contributor, you try to have all the answers. That's your job -- to be an expert, the best at what you do, maybe even the smartest person in the room.

When you are a leader, your job is to have all the questions. You have to be incredibly comfortable looking like the dumbest person in the room. Every conversation you have about a decision, a proposal, or a piece of market information has to be filled with you saying, "What if?" and "Why not?" and "How come?"

Questioning is never enough. You have to make sure your questions unleash debate and raise issues that get action. Remember, however, that just because you are a leader, saying something doesn't mean it will happen.

We've all been guilty at one point or another in our careers of boasting of perfect hindsight. It's a terrible sin. If you don't make sure your questions and concerns are acted upon, it *doesn't count*.

I realize most people don't love the probing process. It's annoying to believe in a product or come into a room with a beautiful presentation only to have it picked apart with questions from the boss.

But that's the job. You want bigger and better solutions. Questions, healthy debate, decisions, and action will get everyone there.

7. Effective leadership management should inspire risk taking and learning by setting the example.

Winning companies embrace risk taking and learning. But in reality, these two concepts often get lip service -- and little else. Too many managers urge their people to try new things and then whack them in the head when they fail. And too many live in not-invented-here worlds of their own making.

If you want your people to experiment and expand their minds, set the example yourself. Consider risk taking. You can create a culture that welcomes risk taking by freely admitting your mistakes and talking about what you've learned from them.

You don't need to be preachy or particularly somber about your errors. In fact, the more humorous and lighthearted you can be about them, the more people will get the message that mistakes aren't fatal.

As for learning, live it yourself. Just because you've the boss doesn't mean you're the source of all knowledge. Whenever I learned about a best practice or better way of giving service from another health care facility, I would come back to re-evaluate our ways of giving services to residents.

There is no edict in the world that will make people take risks or spend their time learning. In most cases, their risk-reward equation just isn't obvious enough. If you want to change that, set the example yourself. You'll love the exciting culture you create and the results you get -- and so will your team.

8. Effective leadership management should celebrate every success when necessary.

What is it about celebrating that makes managers so nervous? Maybe throwing a party doesn't seem professional, or it makes managers worry that they won't look serious to the powers that be, or that, if things get too happy at the office, people will stop working their tails off.

Celebrating makes people feel like winners and creates an atmosphere of recognition and positive energy. Imagine Miami Heat winning the

NBA Championship without champagne spraying everywhere. You just can't! And yet companies win all the time and let it go without so much as a high five. Work is too much a part of life not to recognize moments of achievement. Grab as many as you can. Make a big deal out of them. If you don't, no one will.

In summary, effective leadership should be an *interpersonal* and interacting process in which the leader influences the activities of the followers or the staff toward accomplishment of a goal in a specific situation. Effective leadership sets the pace, goes first, guides and directs the way other people think and act. It is accomplishing goals with and through people.

An effective leadership should be *purposeful*, with reason and always with a clear, attainable, specific, and agreeable goal. An effective leader is interpersonal with social exchange, with a transaction between him or her and the followers. The leader must maintain a relationship that fosters and facilitates healthy communication with the followers.

Effective leadership should be *influential* by offering guidance and direction, thus influencing the ideas and activities of the followers.

I hope this book in many ways has waken you up and energized you as a leader or a potential leader. It is my hope that it has helped you to re-shape your philosophy of what an effective and efficient leader or manager should be. Remember that the leadership DNA or the personality of the leader determines the organization's success or failure. That leadership should build people up by encouragement. That leaders are to give people credit by acknowledgment and give people recognition by gratitude. Leaders are to make things happen in the organization. They are to see opportunities, influence the opinions and actions of others. They are to add values to their subordinates and draw winners to themselves. Leaders are to equip other eagles to lead, provide ideas that help the organization and possess uncommonly great attitude. Finally, leaders should live up to their commitments and show fierce loyalty to the organization and also to their super ordinates -- whoever that may be.

REFERENCES

Allen, James E. (1997). Nursing Home Administration (3rd ed.). New York: Springer Publishing Company.

America's most admired corporations. (1995, March 6). Fortune, p. 66.

Argenti, P.A. (1994). The Portable MBA Desk Reference. New York:. Wiley.

Argyris, C. (1965). Organization and Innovation. Homewood, IL: Irwin.

Barry, Douglas. (2004). *Wisdom for a Young CEO: Incredible Letters & Inspiring Advice from Today's Business Leaders.* Running Press, Philadelphia.

Barnes, John A. & Kennedy, John F. (2005). On Leadership. *The Lessons &Legacy of a President. American Management Association (AMACOM).* New York.

Bennis, W., and Biederman, P. W. (1997). *Organizing Genius.* Reading, Mass.: Addison-Wesley.

Bennis, W., and Nanus, B. (1985). *Leaders.* New York: Harper Collins.

Bennis, W., and Slater, P. (1999). *The Temporary Society.* San Francisco: Jossey-Bass.

Bennis, W., Spreitzer, G.M., and Cummings, T.G., (2001). *The Future of Leadership.* San Francisco: Jossey-Bass.

Bennis, Warren and Nanus, Burt (1985). *Leaders: The Strategies for Taking Charge.* New York: Harper & Row.

Blake, R,R., and Mouton, J.S. (1961). "Reaction to Intergroup Competition under Win-Lose Conditions." Management Science, 7(4):420-425.

Blanchard, Ken & Miller, Mark. (2004). *The Secret: What Great Leaders Know & Do.* Berrett-Koehler Publishers, Inc. San Francisco.

Blanchard, Ken & O'Connor, Michael. (1997). *Managing By Values.* Berrett-Koehler Publishers, San Francisco.

Blumberg, Arthur (July 1959). "Are Teachers Diplomats?" Educational Administration and Supervision, 215-219.

Bounds, G.M. and J.A. Woods. (1998). Supervision. Cincinnati, Ohio: South-Western College Publishing.

Boncarosky, L.D. (1979). " Guidelines to Corrective Discipline," Personnel Journal, 58 (October): 698.

Bullis, Harry A. (1963). What an Executive Should Know About decision Making. Chicago: Dartnell Corporation.

Cartwright, D., and Zander, A. (1968). Group Dynamics: Research and Theory, New York: Harper & Row.

Cloud, Henry, (2006). *Integrity*. Harper Collins Publisher. New York.

Cohen, A. R., Fink, S. L., Gadon, H., and Willits, R.D. (1988). Effective Behavior in Organizations. Homewood, IL: Irwin.

Conger, Jay and Benjamin, Beth (1999). *Building Leaders: How Successful Companies Develop the Next Generation.* San Francisco: Jossey-Bass.

Cosier, R.A., and Schwenk, C. R. (1990). "Agreement and Thinking Alike: Ingredients for Poor Decisions." Academic Management Extract, 4(1): 69-74.

Covey, Stephen R. (1990). *The 7 Habits of Highly Effective People: Restoring the character ethic.* A Fireside Book Publishing Company, New York.

Croce, Pat. (2004). *Lead or Get Off the Pot: Seven Secrets of a Self-made Leader.* Simon & Schuster, N.Y.

Dale, E. (1978). Management: Theory and practice (4th ed.). New York: McGraw hill.

Decker, P. J. (1982). Healthcare Management Microtraining. St. Louis, MO: Decker and Associates.

Deutsch, M. (1968). "The Effects of Cooperation and Competition upon Group Process." In: Group Dynamics: Research and Theory.

Drucker, P.F. (1954). The Practice of management. New York: Harper and Row, 252, 353-364.

Drucker, Peter F. (2002). Managing in the Next Society, New York: Harper & Row Publishers.

Drucker, Peter F. (1999). Management Challenges for 21st Century. New York: Harper & Row Publishers.

Drucker, Peter F. (1998). On the Profession of Management. New York: Harper & Row Publishers.

Festinger, L., Schacter, S., and Black, K. (1950). Social Pressures in Informal Groups: A Study of a Housing Project. New York: Harper & Row.

Fiedler, F.E. (1967). A Theory of Leadership Effectiveness. New York: McGraw-Hill.

Franklin, Benjamin, quoted in Bullis, What an Executive Should Know, 19-21.

Gatewood, R.D., and Field, H.S. (1990). Human Resource Selection. Chicago: Dryden.

Gible, C.A. (July 1947). "The Principles and Trials of Leadership." The Journal of Abnormal and Social Psychology.

Gold Hammer, R. (1980). Clinical Supervision. (2nd ed.). New York: Holt, Rinehart Winston.

Goleman, Daniel (2002). *Working with Emotional Intelligence* New York: Bantam, 317. For an interesting exchange about leadership and practical intelligence, see Robert Sternberg and Victor Vroom, "The Person Versus the Situation in Leadership," *The Leadership Quarterly* 13, no. 3 (June 2002): 301-321.

Greenleaf, Robert K., (2002). *Servant Leadership*. Paulist Press. New York.

Griffiths, Daniel (1969). Quoted in Fred D. Carver and Thomas J. Sergiovanni, Organizations and Human Behavior: Focus on Schools. New York: McGraw-Hill Book Company, 140.

Gulick,L. & Lyndall. (Eds.). (1937). Papers on the science of administration. New York: Institute of Public Administration.

Hamel, G., & Prahalad, C.K. (1994). Competing for the future. Boston, MA: Harvard Business School Press.

Hampton et al., (1973). Organizational Behavior, 285, 286, 333.

Harkins, S., Latane, B. and Williams, L. (1980). "Social Loafing: Allocating Effort or 'Taking It Easy,' "Journal of Experimental Social Psychology, 16:457-465.

Heifetz, Ronald A. and Linsky, Mary, (2002). *Leadership on the Line: Staying Alive Through the Dangers of Leading.* Boston: Harvard Business School Press, 164).

Hemphil J. K. (1949). Situational Factors in Leadership. Columbus, Ohio. Ohio State University, 30-33.

Hershey, P., and Blanchard, K. (1988). Management of Organizational Behavior: Utilizing Human Resources. 5th ed. Englewood Cliffs, NJ: Prentice-Hall.

Holy Bible. *New King James Version* (1995) Max Lucado Ed. Word Bibles, Dallas

Homans, G. (1961). Social Behavior: Its Elementary Forms. New York: Harcourt Brace.

House, R. J., and Mitchell, T.R. (1974). "Path-Goal Theory of Leadership." Journal of Contemporary Business, 3:81.

Hoy and Miskel, Educational Administration, 300.

Iacocca, Lee and Novak, William, (1984). Iacocca: An Autobiography. Bantam Books: New York.

Ivancevich, J. M., and Glueck, W. F. (1986). Foundations of Personnel/ Human Resource Management. 3rd ed. Plano, TX: Business Publications.

Jackson, J. (1960). The Organization and its communication problems. In A. Grimshaw & J. W. Hennessey, Jr. (Eds.).Organizational behavior: Cases and Readings. New York: McGraw-Hill.

Janis, I.L. (1982). Groupthink: Psychological Studies of Policy Decisions and Fiascos. (2nd ed.). Boston: Houghton Mifflin.

Jenkins, R.L., and Henderson, R.L. (1984). "Motivating the staff: What Nurses Expect from Their Supervisors." Nursing Management, 15(2):13.

Johnson, H.J. & Hodger, B.J. (1970). Management and Organizational Behavior. New York: John Wiley & Sons.

Kanter, Rosabeth Moss (1983). *The Change Masters: Innovation & Entrepreneurship in the American Corporation.* New York: Simon and Schuster.

Kast, F.E., and Rosenzweig, J.D. (1985). Organization and Management, (4th ed.). New York: McGraw-Hill Book Company.

Katz, D., & Kahn, R. L. (1967). The Social Psychology of Organizations. New York: Wiley.

Katz, D., and Kahn, R. (1978). The Social Psychology of Organizations. New York: Wiley.

Kelley, R.E. (1988). "In Praise of Followers." Harvard Business Review, 88(6): 142-148.

Kellerman, Barbara. (2004). *"Bad Leadership: What It is, How It Happens, Why It Matters.* Harvard Business School Press.

Kotter, John P. (1990). *A Force for Change: How Leadership Differs from Management.* New York: Free Press.

Ketter, J.P. (1982). The General Managers. New York: Free Press.

Kriegel, R.J. (1991). If It Ain't Broke. New York: Warner.

Lall, Bernard M. & Lall, Geeta Rani (1979). *New Dynamic Leadership: Contemporary Leadership Concepts.* Geetanjali Publishers, U.S.A.

Latham, G.P., and Wexley, K. N. (1980). Increasing Productivity through Performance Appraisal. Reading, MA: Addison-Wesley.

Lawler, E.E. (1986). High Involvement Management, San Francisco, CA: Jossey Bass.

Levey, S., & Loomba, N.P. (1984). Health Care Administration: A Managerial Perspective (2nd ed.). New York: Lippincott.

Levine, J.M., and Moreland, R.L. (1990). "Progress in Small Group Research." Annual Review of Psychology, 41:585-634.

Likert, R. (1961). New Patterns of Management. New York: McGraw-Hill.

Marks, J.R. Stoops, E. and King-Stoops, J. (1971). Handbooks of Educational Supervision Boston: Allyn and Bacon.

Marvin, Philip (1971). Developing Decision for Action. Homewood, Illinois: Dow Jones-Irwin, 177, 178.

Maxwell, John. (2005). *The 360 Degree Leader: Developing Your Influence from Anywhere in the Organization.* Nelson Business Publishers.

McCafferty, R. M. (1988). Employee Benefit Programs: A Total Compensation Perspective. Boston: PWS-Kent.

McGregory, Douglas. (1960). The Human Side of Enterprise. Cambridge: MIT Press 222-227.

Mintzberg, H. (1979). The Structure of Organizations: A Synthesis of the Research. Englewood Cliffs, NJ: Prentice-Hall.

Mitchell, T.R., and Larson, J.R., (1987). People in Organizations. 3rd ed. New York: McGraw-Hill.

Mitchell, T.R. (1974). "Expectancy Models of Job Satisfaction, Occupational Preference, and Effort: A Theoretical, Methodological and Empirical Appraisal." Psychological Bulleting, 81: 1096.

Moore, R., et al. (1982). "On the Scene: Quality Circles at Barnes Hospital." Nursing Administration Quarterly 6:3

Morell, R.W. (1969). Managements Ends and Means. San Francisco: Chandler Publishing Company, 75

Morphet, Edgar, & Johns, Roe Reller, Theodore. *Educational Organization and Administration Concepts, Practices and Issues.* (Eaglewood Cliffs, New essey: Prince-Hall, 1974), 106-124.

Murninghan, K. (1981). "Group Decision: What Strategies to Use?" Management Review, 70: 55-61.

Murphy, K.R., and Cleveland, J.N. (1991). Performance Appraisal. Boston: Allyn and Bacon.

Nelson, Bob & Economy, Peter. (2005). *The Management Bible.* John Wiley & Sons, Inc. New Jersey.

Newman, W. (1956). " Overcoming Obstacles to effective Delegation." Management Review, 45(1):36-41.

O'Toole, James. (1995). *Leading Change: Overcoming the Ideology of Comfort and the Tranny of Custom.* San Fransisco: Jossey-Bass, p.2.

Ouchi, W. (1981). Theory Z: How American Business Can Meet the Japanese Challenge. Reading, MA: Addison-Wesley.

Patten, T.H. (1979). "Team Building Part 1: Designing the Intervention." Personnel, 56 (1): 11-21.

Peters, Thomas J. and Waterman, Robert H. Jr. (1982). *In Search of Excellence: Lessons from America's Best-Run Companies.* New York: Warner.

Peters, T., & Austin, N. (1985). A Passion for Excellence: The Leadership Difference. New York: Random House.

Peters, T. (1987). Thriving on Chaos. New York: Harper and Row.

Pfeffer, J., & Salanick, G.R. (1978). The External Control of Organizations. New York: Harper and Row.

Pigors, P.J.W. (1935). Leadership or Domination? Boston: Houghton Mifflin Co. 16.

Plunkett, Supervision (1997). The Direction of People, 25.

Poteet, G. (1984). " Delegation Strategies: A Must for the Nurse Executive." Journal of Nursing Administration. 14(9):18-21.

Pressman, J.L. & Wildavsky, A.B. (1974). Implementation. Berkely: University of California Press.

Psychiatrist Michael Weiner has this view of evil, as cited by Sharon Begley, "The Roots of Evil," *Newsweek*, 21 May 2002, 32.

Rebore, R.W. (1995). Personnel Administration in Education: A management approach. (4th Ed.), Boston: Allyn and Bacon

Rhodes, S.R., and Steers, R. M. (1990) Managing Employee Absenteeism. Reading, MA: Addison-Wesley.

Roberts, W. (1990). Leadership Secrets of Attila the Hun. New York: Warner Books.

Robey, D. (1982). Designing Organizations. Homewood. IL: Irwin.

Ronan, W.W., Latham, G.P., and Kinney, S. B. (1973). Effects of Goal Setting and Supervision on Worker Behavior in an Industrial Situation." Journal of Applied Psychology, 58: 302.

Sherif, M. (1967). Group Conflict and Cooperation: Their Social Psychology. Boston: Routledge & Kegan Paul.

Sherman, A. et al. (1998). Managing Human Resources. 11th ed. Cincinnati, Ohio: South-Western College Publishing.

Singleton, J.W. *Decision Making.* Education Canada, September, 1972.

Singh, D. (2005). Effective Management of Long-Term Care Facilities. Sudbury, Massachusetts: Jones and Bartlett Publishers.

Smith, H. L., Reinow, F.D., and Reid, R.A. (1984). "Japanese Management: Implications for Nursing Administration." Journal of Nursing Administration

Spradley, B.W. (1990). Community Health Nursing: Concepts and Practice (3rd Ed.),

Glenview, IL: Scott, Foresman/Little, Brown Higher Education.

Steers, R.M. (1984). Introduction to Organizational Behavior. (2nd ed.). Glenview, IL: Scott, Foresman.

Stogdill, R.M. (1974). Handbook of Leadership: A Survey of the Literature. New York: Free Press.

Sullivan, Eleanor J. & Decker, Phillip J. 3rd ed. (1992). Effective Management In Nursing. Addison-Wesley Publishing Company.

Summers, H. Lawrence. (October 12, 2001) *Installation Address of Lawrence H. Summers."* Harvard University.

Tead, Ordway, (1935). The Art of Leadership. New York: McGraw-Hill Book Company, 20

Terry, G. R. (1969). Principles of Management. Homewood, IL: Irwin.

The failure by South Carolina governor Jim Hodges to communicate during Hurricane Floyd resulted in a monumental traffic jam. "Traffic Backs Up for Miles as Coastal Dwellers flee Island," *St.*

Louis Post-Dispatch, 16 September 1999, A9. See also Leigh Strope, "Hodges Said He Should Control Emergency Response," Associated Press State and Local Wire,

1 October 1999; and David Firestone, "Hurricane Floyd: The Overview," New York Times, 16 September 1999, A1.

Thompson, Stewart, (1975). The Age of Manager Is Over. Homewood, Illinois Dow Jones-Irwin.

Thompson, Victor, (1977). Modern Organization 2nd ed. New York: University of Alabama Press.

Tichy, Noel with Cohen, Eli (1997). *The Leadership Engine: How Winning Companies Build Leaders at Every Level.* New York: Harper Business.

Titus, C.A. (1950). The Process of Leadership. Dubuque, Iowa: William C. Brown Company, 352.

Townsend J.E., Davis, W.E. and Haacker R.W. (2007). "The Principles of Health Care Administration." Bosssier City, LA: Professional Printing & Publishing, Inc.

Tuckman, B.W., and Jensen, M.A. (1977). "Stages of Small Group Development Revisited." Group and Organizational Studies, 2: 419-427.

Tuchman, Barbara, (1984). The Match of Folly: *Troy to Vietnam* New York: Ballentine, 7.

Van de Ven, A.H., and Delbecq, A.L. (1974). "The Effectiveness of Nominal, Delphi, and Interacting Group Decision Making Processes." Academic Management Journal, 17(4): 605-621.

Vroom, V.H., and Jago, A.G. (1988). The New Leadership Englewood Cliffs, NJ: Prentice-Hall.

Weber, A Clarence, (1961). Fundamentals of Educational Leadership. New York: Exposition Press. 67-82, 230.

Welch, Jack & Suzy. *Winning.* (2005). Harpe Business New York, N.Y. pp. 61-80.

Welch, J.F. (December 13, 1993). A Master Class in Radical Change. Future, p. 83.

Whetten, D., and Cameron, K. (1984). Developing Management Skills. Glenwood, IL: Scott, Foresman.

Wrapp, H.E. (1984). Good Managers Don't Make Policy Decisions. Harvard Business Review, 84,(4).

Yukl, G.A., and Taber, T. (1983). "The Effective Use of Managerial Power." Personnel (March-April):60(2):37.

Zaleznik, A., Christensen, C.R., and Roethlisberger, F.J. (1958). The Motivation,Productivity and Satisfaction of Workers. Boston: Harvard University Business School.

Webster's 9th New Collegiate Dictionary (2006). Springfield, MA: Merriam-Webster.

White, E.G. Manuscript, (1907).

White, E.G. (1907), pp. 9, 10. Individual Responsibility and Christian Unity, Jan. 1907

White E.G. Manuscript, (1902, 140).

White, E.G. (1932) Medical Ministry

White, E.G. Prophets and Kings, pp. 30-31.

White, E.G. Letter, (1903).

White, E.G. Letter, (1907).

White, E.G. (1888), Letter 3, p. 4. January 10.

White, E.G. (1896), Letter 4, pp. 13, 15, 16, July 1, To Men in Responsible Positions.

White, E.G. (1885), Letter 12, Oct. 28, To Butler and Haskell.

White, E.G. (1898), Letter 39, p. 13 March 27, to Brethren Woods and Miller.

White, E.G. (1892), Letter 20, October, 17, 1892 to J.H. Kellogg.

White, E.G. (1897), Letter 49, Sept. 1897, Workers in our Institutions.

White, E.G. Testimonies, Vol. 3: pp. 23, 497.

White, E.G. Testimonies, Vol. 4, pp. 310-311.

White, E.G. Testimonies, Vol. 5, p. 423.

While, E.G. Testimonies, Vol. 9: 278.

White, E.G. Testimonies to Ministers, pp. 323-4.

Wiles, Kimball, and Lovell, John T. (1975) Supervision for Better Schools. Englewood Cliffs, New Jersey: Prentice-Hall, 99.

INDEX

ABOUT THE AUTHOR

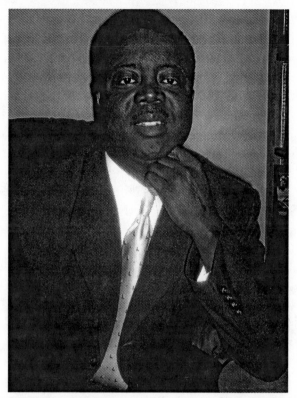

Michael Adewale Adeniyi, Ph.D. was born at Ode Lemo, Ogun State, Nigeria in September 08 1961 to Chief and Mrs. Balogun Samuel and Rachael Adeniyi. He is the third child of four sons and two daughters. He attended Ode Lemo Anglican Primary School in 1967.

In September of 1976, he was admitted into the Baptist Secondary Modern School, Igboho, Oyo State, Nigeria and graduated in 1978. The same year he got his first employment as the general secretary at the National Missionary Seminary Of St. Paul, (NMSSP) Iperu Remo, Ogun State, Nigeria, under the leadership of Rev. Father James M. Sheering of Ireland.

In September 1980, he was admitted to the Adventist Seminary of West Africa (ASWA). In summers of 1984 and 1985, he became literature evangelist in Nigeria and in summers of 1986 to 1990 to Skandinaviska Bokforlaget, Sweden.

He graduated in June 1988 with Bachelors of Arts in Religion/Business and went to NewBold College, Britain, where he graduated in June 1990 with Masters of Arts in Education. He left United Kingdom for the United States of America and graduated in December 1995 with Associate in Applied Science - Nursing and in May 2000 with Doctoral Degree in Educational Administration and Supervision.

Between 1995 and 2000, he worked as staff and charge nurse of various hospitals, nursing homes, and behavioral centers. In 1998 he and his wife became licensees and administrators of Wholistic Home Health Adult Foster Care and Assisted Living Facility, Inc. Niles, MI. He is an Adjunct Lecturer in the department of Humanities and Social Sciences at Southwestern Michigan College since 2003 and Ferris State University since 2006. He is a certified instructor of First Aid, CPR, and AED with American Red Cross.

He is the Director of Coronary Health Improvement Project, (CHIP) and Health and Temperance Director of the First Seventh-Day Adventist Church, South Bend, since 2003.

He was president of two Nigerian non-profit organizations: Nigerian Family Fellowship (NFF) 1993 to 1998 and Nigerian Association of Michiana (NAM) 2002 to 2005 and actively involved in the member's welfare. He is currently the Public Relation Officer for the Nigerian Adventists in North America (NANA) Michigan and Indiana chapter.

He was awarded "The All Nigeria Conference of Principals of Secondary Schools (ANCOPSS) Merit", February 2006.

He is a member of the American Red Cross, Michigan Assisted Living Association, Michigan and Indiana Nurses Associations, American Higher Education and Leadership Association, and Michigan Long Term Care Partnership.

He and his wife Grace were blessed with four beautiful grown up children: Mary, Stephen (deceased), Andrew, and Michelle (Valentina). The family reside in Granger, Indiana, U.S.A.

BOOK SUMMARY

Effective Leadership Management is about theory and practice of effective leadership management. It is about what a leader or manager does to bring about staff efficiency and effectiveness. A leader or a manager is effective when he or she brings about the desired results for the organization by using different approaches to the development of personal and interpersonal effectiveness of the staff by daily decision making, staffing, planning, forecasting, nurturing, coaching, directing, organizing, marketing, encouraging and controlling quality.

Effective Leadership Management emphasizes leadership as the intersection of character, knowledge, skill and desire. People who become leaders tend to have qualities or abilities such as competencies, know their field, their industry and their discipline. They should be building relationship or forming an alliance, networking, or partnerships with others. To lead successfully, a leader must have the third ingredient of character with integrity. This is not necessarily performance but morals and ethics.

Effective Leadership Management styles are achievable by using mixtures of different styles as situation arises. Each leader has to choose style(s) that suits his or her personality and that best represents the values of the organization. In all, a leader has to be transparent with all daily dealings, communicates effectively, be honest with staff members, showing an unbending integrity, at the same time be knowledgeable or skillful about the tasks at hand, and be easy to follow. When an employee is encouraged, motivated and positively appraised, his or her performance will be enhanced.

This book strongly emphasizes theory Z by Dr. Ouchi in which a management or leadership style focuses on a strong company philosophy, a distinctive corporate culture, long-range staff development, and consensus decision making. When decisions and policies that relate to customers are being made by an organization, it is important to understand that others such as customers, community, staff, suppliers and stake holders opinions should be considered. This is called a holistic view approach to decision making.

We are becoming a nation dominated by large and small institutions - churches, businesses, governments, labor unions, universities - it is my hope that every reader will find this book useful either as a clergy, school principal or university president, hospital or nursing home administrator, nurse manager or departmental head, company owners or CEO that an effective and efficient leader or manager in the 21st century cannot lead or manage alone by skills or knowledge, but with styles, character, personality, serving, and by example.

Printed in the United States
114570LV00002B/103-135/A